Michele is a friend I absolutely adore and trust to speak truth over deep places in my life when I need a confidant. If you have ever felt burdened with unanswered questions and prayers, this book is a must-read. God's truths are woven through Michele's many beautiful words and heartbreaking stories. She is wise. She is funny. She helps her reader find God's comfort, love, and revelation in the midst of hardship. And best of all, she offers up bouquets of the sweetest grace on every page.

—Lysa TerKeurst, author, *New York Times* bestselling *The Best Yes*; president, Proverbs 31 Ministries

While this looks like a book, it's not. It's actually a life preserver disguised as a book. Hearing Michele's story helped me to understand more clearly my own story and to connect it to the even bigger story of God's fierce, persistent, and gracious love. It made me laugh, cry, and ponder anew the mystery of suffering and the meaning of life.

—Michael Hyatt, *New York Times* bestselling author; former CEO, Thomas Nelson Publishers

What a book! Mesmerizing, funny, heartbreaking, redemptive. A messy story full of honesty and hope. My heart felt like it grew bigger and wiser reading this finely crafted tome.

—Patsy Clairmont, author, *Twirl ... A Fresh Spin at Life*; Women of Faith speaker

Undone mended my heart. Michele's honest words soothed my deepest fears that I was the only mom/wife/friend who battled a messy, confusing life. She tackles her story with the kind of authenticity that lets Jesus shine through the broken places.

—Mary DeMuth, author, *Thin Places: A Memoir*

Michele Cushatt is an exceptional writer who weaves humor and honesty in a powerful way that helps people face some of the hardest issues that life brings their way. Her heartwarming, inspiring story, *Undone*, helps us more clearly see through difficult circumstances and recognize the hand of God in the midst of it all. Don't miss *Undone*. It is a book that leads to life fully alive.

—Ken Davis, author; comedian; inspirational speaker

God's great strength is most evident in our great weakness. In no other story I've read in the past five years is that statement more evident than in Michele Cushatt's *Undone*. Every page is doused with the grace of God shared through a woman who has been broken wide open so that his presence is unmistakable in her life. You will walk away convinced that your own messy faith, lived in imperfect ways, is enough. A must-read

—Kathi Lipp, author, *The Cure for th*
Trying Harder and Start Living Braver

Do yourself a massive favor and read this book! I cannot recommend it highly enough. Michele is one of the most gifted communicators I've ever met, but more than that, she's one of the most Jesus-filled people I've ever known. Michele's story will inspire you, move you, and leave you feeling empowered that you too can face overwhelming odds and unknowns with courage and bravery.

—Crystal Paine, founder of MoneySavingMom.com; author, *New York Times* bestselling *Say Goodbye to Survival Mode*

What do you do when life doesn't turn out the way you always thought it would? Reading this masterfully written and poignant book, I found myself immediately captivated by both Michele's personal story and her ability to tell it. Once I started reading, I found I couldn't put it down. In the end, it offered hope amid the messiness of life and provided a powerful reminder that while God doesn't promise a life free of pain, he does promise never to let us go. *Undone* is a must-read—one of the best books I've read all year.

—Ruth Soukup, founder, LivingWellSpendingLess.com; author, *Living Well, Spending Less: Twelve Secrets of the Good Life*

The hardest things in life have a way of showing up unexpectedly, as do the most beautiful and breathtaking. Through Michele's story, I found mine. Through her remembering, I was reminded. Reminded how God has shown up when I least expected him. How comfort and peace have pulled up close when I felt alone. How strength came in the most unexpected ways. If you feel like you're coming undone, read this book and let Michele's words awaken the hope and courage your heart needs today!

—Renee Swope, author, bestselling *A Confident Heart*; radio cohost, *Everyday Life with Lysa and Renee*; Proverbs 31 Ministries

Reading Michele Cushatt's memoir, *Undone*, left me . . . well, *undone:* amazed at the trials and testings of one woman, yet in awe of the tenacity and tenderness of our God. Michele's pilgrimage through life wasn't at all what she'd expected. But it turned out to be just what she needed. Every new twist. Each unwanted turn. Her rollercoaster ride of emotional and physical pain changed her. Reading her story will change you too. This book will empower you to more trustingly rely on God, who promises to travel not only with but ***in*** all who cling to him during every leg of life's journey.

—Karen Ehman, Proverbs 31 Ministries speaker; author, *Let. It. Go* and *Keep It Shut*

Michele's life gives me courage—and hope—to live my life. Most of us—all of us?—think we are the only ones. The only ones stunned and surprised by the life we are suddenly living. But we're not the only ones. Each of us is called to be open to God's unexpected invitation into an unimaginable calling of brokenness that actually makes us beautiful. Through telling her story, Michele helps us say yes. I say yes.

—Elisa Morgan, speaker; author, *The Beauty of Broken*

Undone undid me! This is a deeply moving, powerfully tender story, an encouraging God-salve for the raw soul

—Marilyn Meberg, author; speaker; Women of Faith original speaker

For any woman who struggles with a life that has morphed into something between soap opera and sitcom, who has frantically tried to patch something together while it's coming apart, who wants so badly to do it all perfectly but gets overwhelmed by the reality of her humanity, welcome to *Undone*. Beautifully told, vulnerably crafted. Reading Michele's unfolding story is like finding an understanding friend at the juncture where panic meets surrender and peace.

—Becky Johnson, coauthor, *We Laugh, We Cry, We Cook* and *Nourished: A Search for Health, Happiness, and a Full Night's Sleep*

This is a hopeful, heartfelt memoir about finding the hidden beauty in the midst of life's greatest struggles. In Michele's story, you will see your own story—and find something beautiful to hold onto.

—Jeff Goins, author, *The Art of Work*

As you read this beautiful memoir, you will find Michele crawling right into your heart. You will identify with her pain, be humbled by her courage, and grab onto her hope. Long after you've turned the last page, you will be dwelling on what Michele's life has taught you about yours.

—Dr. Juli Slattery, psychologist; founder, Authentic Intimacy

Through the fire, Michele Cushatt emerges whole, lifted, and shining. What a beautiful journey to share. A courageous testament to holding fast to God's hand, regardless of life's heat and hurdles, and never letting go. Encouraging and beautiful.

—Patricia Raybon, award-winning author, *I Told the Mountain to Move*, *My First White Friend*, and *Undivided*

Undone is like a conversation with an old beloved friend, where you feel oh-so-honored to be entrusted with their overwhelming fears, deepest desires, and unquenchable hope for the future. Michele's memoir is a brilliant and beautiful account of resting in God through every trial, and a clear vision of what it means to willfully embrace the wild turns of life.

—Shannon Ethridge, international speaker; life/relationship coach; author, bestselling Every Woman's Battle series

With an honesty that is truly inspiring, Michele Cushatt has written a brave account of her own complicated life. Her book is a gift and constant companion to anyone who has gone through the trials of life and relied on an unshakable faith. For anyone who yearns to understand where God is in the midst of this crazy life, I cannot recommend *Undone* highly enough.

—Brenda Warner, author, *First Things First*

I adore Michele's writing and her pure and courageous heart. The grace she's traveled is nothing short of amazing. In *Undone*, Michele invites us into a life turned upside-down and the creative God who can achieve in our hearts and minds what we don't always think is possible—an unshakeable faith and a gutsy resolve that transforms our perspective of what a life well-lived truly is.

—Carrie Wilkerson, author, *The Barefoot Executive*; CarrieWilkerson.com

I knew Michele Cushatt has amazing artistry with words. What I didn't know was how *Undone* would settle into my bones, with startling impact. Michele has spoken for all humanity in its pages, pointing to the Master Creator, reminding us of our imperfect lives and how they are beautiful, no matter the unexpected struggle. Bravo, Michele, bravo. I'll be reading this again.

—Lisa Whittle, author, *Whole* and *I Want God*

I laughed and cried as I read this gripping page-turning account of Michele's life. Her honest struggles and deep faith created within me a desire to do more—to *be* more—for God. I unreservedly recommend *Undone* to anyone who needs a healthy dose of God-infused inspiration.

—Lorraine Pintus, international speaker; writing coach; author, *Jump Off the Hormone Swing*

In her book, *Undone*, my beautiful friend Michele Cushatt has left me just that, undone. Her courage to be real gives all of us permission to remove our masks of perfectionism and embrace our authentic, work-in-progress, undone selves. I *love* this book and the freedom it brings!

—Yvette Maher, executive pastor, New Life Church, Colorado Springs

Undone is not only compelling and riveting in its content; it's deeply uncompromised in its declaration. For no matter the circumstance we find ourselves in, we are seen by a lovesick Father who never takes his eyes off of us. In all the complicated realties of our brokenness, with intoxicating love, he whispers, *I am with you; I see you; you are mine.*

—Tammy Maltby, television and radio host; author, *The God Who Sees You*

Undone

Undone

A MEMOIR

A STORY OF
MAKING PEACE
WITH AN
UNEXPECTED LIFE

Michele Cushatt

ZONDERVAN

Undone
Copyright © 2015 by Michele Cushatt

This title is also available as a Zondervan ebook. Visit www.zondervan.com/ebooks.

Requests for information should be addressed to:
Zondervan, *3900 Sparks Dr. SE, Grand Rapids, Michigan 49546*

Library of Congress Cataloging-in-Publication Data

Cushatt, Michele, 1971–
Undone : a memoir : finding peace in an unexpected life / Michele Cushatt.
pages cm
Includes bibliographical references.
ISBN 978-0-310-33978-6 (softcover)
1. Cushatt, Michele, 1971- 2. Christian biography. I. Title.
BR1725.C848A3 2015
287.092–dc23 [B] 2014016732

All Scripture quotations, unless otherwise indicated, are taken from the Holy Bible, *New International Version®, NIV®*. Copyright © 1973, 1978, 1984, 2011 by Biblica, Inc.® Used by permission. All rights reserved worldwide.

Any Internet addresses (websites, blogs, etc.) and telephone numbers in this book are offered as a resource. They are not intended in any way to be or imply an endorsement by Zondervan, nor does Zondervan vouch for the content of these sites and numbers for the life of this book.

All rights reserved. No part of this publication may be reproduced, stored in a retrieval system, or transmitted in any form or by any means—electronic, mechanical, photocopy, recording, or any other—except for brief quotations in printed reviews, without the prior permission of the publisher.

Published in association with the literary agency of Wolgemuth & Associates, Inc.

The names and identifying characteristics of some of the people in this book have been changed to protect their privacy. While this is a work of nonfiction and the author has selected what to include, it is based on her own perspective and recollection of events.

Cover design: Jamie DeBruyn
Cover photography: © Katrin Ray Shumakov / Getty Images®
Interior design: Beth Shagene
Interior photography: © Katrin Ray Shumakov / Getty Images®, © lissart / iStockphoto®

First printing January 2015 / Printed in the United States of America

To Troy,
Tyler, Ryan, Jacob,
Princess, Peanut, and Jack,
the splashes of color on my canvas.
And to the Artist,
who weaves all things together
into a breathtaking whole.
I'm undone.

Contents

Who shall separate us from the love of Christ? Shall trouble or hardship or persecution or famine or nakedness or danger or sword?... No, in all these things we are more than conquerors through him who loved us. For I am convinced that neither death nor life, neither angels nor demons, neither the present nor the future, nor any powers, neither height nor depth, nor anything else in all creation, will be able to separate us from the love of God that is in Christ Jesus our Lord.

—ROMANS 8:35, 37–39

CHAPTER 1

The Phone Call

Little by little we human beings are confronted with situations that give us more and more clues that we are not perfect.

—**FRED ROGERS**, *Mr. Rogers' Neighborhood: Thoughts for All Ages*

IT STARTED WITH A PHONE CALL.

November 23, the Tuesday morning before Thanksgiving Day. The doctor's voice caught me by surprise, his words even more so: "Michele, it's not good."

Gut punch.

I didn't expect to find out I had cancer two days before Thanksgiving. Some holidays should be off limits. Just saying.

The breakfast dishes sat in the sink, cereal bowls and coffee mugs dropped in my hurry to get kids to school. My husband, Troy, already late, hustled through the house grabbing computer bag and coat for a full day of customer appointments. Bread crumbs from hastily assembled sack lunches lingered on the counter, the newspaper sprawled across the table. All marks of an ordinary day in our home.

Only today was no longer ordinary. Even as I sat in the living room chair, the phone in one hand and my forehead in the other, I knew my life would never be the same.

Six days before, after doing a biopsy, Dr. Francis had assured me I had no reason to fear. "It's nothing, Michele. Nothing. But we'll do the biopsy anyway." Yes, he'd said that. Multiple times. So I didn't worry, because I had no need to.

Michele, it's not good.

All the fear the doctor had stayed the week before now filled me with panic. I couldn't breathe, felt like I was drowning.

I'd turned thirty-nine only a few short months before. Too young. I thought of my three teenage boys without a mother. My husband without a wife. I pictured the dreams I wouldn't reach, all the events I would miss. The cross-country meets, homecoming pictures, and high school graduations. In a moment, cancer rewrote my life as a worst-case scenario. I hated it.

At different times in my life, I'd imagined getting a phone call like this, even wondered how I'd respond. Every time, I pictured myself a pillar of strength, absorbing bad news with a sweep of the hand and a stoic grace, an actress's well-executed theatrics. It seems silly now, my imagination, compared with reality. Cancer has nothing of Hollywood in it.

Officially, Dr. Francis said, cancer of the tongue. A rare, squamous-cell carcinoma typically found in smokers. Only I wasn't a smoker, had never been. Regardless of how many times I asked, he couldn't explain it, couldn't tell me why. Instead, he assigned me to a surgeon who later scheduled a PET scan and a December surgery, a partial glossectomy to remove a section of my tongue. After that, results would be analyzed and a treatment plan would be created.

Fear and unknowns marked Thanksgiving that year. Waiting and worrying, crying and praying. A hundred times I've tried to put words to that time. Like trying to explain the deep end of the ocean to a bird who has known only the feel of the sky. How do I capture that first day, my kids at school and my husband at work, when I cried at home alone, curled up in my bedroom closet? How do I describe telling my youngest boy when he came home from school, the one who still cuddled with his mama at night, and then holding him and wiping tears from his eyes? How do I give justice to the sleepless nights and panic-filled days while I waited, waited, waited for PET scan and pathology results? At six o'clock I woke up to a life I loved. By eight thirty it was gone.

The phone call with Dr. Francis ended almost as quickly as it began, like a tornado ripping through a town in just minutes but changing the landscape forever.

"Any questions?" he asked.

Of course I had questions! Terrifying, consuming ones. What if it has already spread? How soon will we know a prognosis? Will I be able to talk normally once I heal? Is my speaking career over? What about my boys? What should I tell them?

Will I live?

"No, I'm okay."

Only I wasn't.

I hung up the phone. And fell completely apart.

PART 1

Life and Death

CHAPTER 2

Thanksgiving

Of course it is different when the thing happens to oneself, not to others, and in reality, not in imagination.

—C. S. LEWIS, *A Grief Observed*

FOR AS LONG AS I CAN REMEMBER, THANKSGIVING HAS BEEN MY favorite holiday. The pinnacle of every year.

Until the year cancer joined my family at the table.

I tried to stay festive, buy the turkey, whip up pies and side dishes, all while smiling and laughing as expected. But behind the charade of activity, I felt myself crumbling.

That first day proved the most difficult. I hung up the phone with Dr. Francis as Troy rushed out the door to work. An empty house. I tried to do the dishes but couldn't stand still. I pulled out my Bible but couldn't read. Fear made me inconsolable. The silence screamed.

From the time I sat in a kindergarten Sunday school class, I've been told to talk to God about these things first. Call him up on the heavenly 911 and "pour out my lament" like David or Isaiah. Certainly my heart called out to him while I paced from room to room trying to find a distraction. But I couldn't form any coherent prayer other than "Help me." Even then, more silence in reply.

So I called Kate, the friend with whom I'd shared countless cups of tea. She always seemed to know the right thing to say to a friend in crisis. But she didn't answer. I thought about leaving a message, but what to say?

Call me. I have cancer.

Not voicemail material. Besides, speaking would've breached the dam holding back a torrent of emotion. I was afraid I'd start crying and never stop.

I tried another friend, Robbie, the one who always knows how to make me laugh. I needed to laugh. As long as I've known her, she's been strong, feisty, and optimistic. She wouldn't break down at my news, wouldn't fall apart in a panic. I didn't need any more of that. Knowing her, she'd talk a little smack, shake me by the shoulders, and dole out a plateful of faith and perspective.

I couldn't dial fast enough. But again, no answer.

For the third time that morning, I hung up the phone to an empty house. Fear spread like a flood, drowning me. I wanted to run but had nowhere to go.

Why? Of all days, why can't I find someone to help me?

My terror finally pushed me to my bedroom closet. To pray.

I don't remember what I said, and I'm quite sure it wasn't anything worthy of the pages of the Psalms. It was more groans than words, more tears than testimony. I fell facedown on the carpet, the closet door shut and darkness enveloping me, and uttered a prayer of panic.

Father God, help me. Please, help. I want to live!

Somewhere at the tail end of that prayer I made a request. Desperate for human company, for some kind of physical presence to ease my fear, I asked God to bring someone—anyone—

to sit with me. Didn't matter if it was a phone call or a visitor on my front step.

Please don't make me endure today alone.

I listened for the doorbell. Waited. Strained to hear. Nothing. Only silence. Defeated, convinced of my aloneness, I pulled myself off the floor and headed downstairs to work on the breakfast dishes.

Only a few minutes passed.

Then my cell phone rang.

I felt a surge of hope, anticipating Kate's or Robbie's name on the caller ID.

Neither. Instead, Christine.

Christine and I weren't really friends. At least, not anymore. At one time we'd been part of the same circles and spent regular time together. But for reasons I didn't understand, she'd fallen out of love with our friendship. With me. It'd been nearly a year since we'd last spoken or seen each other. I couldn't imagine why she'd be calling.

"Hello, this is Michele."

"Michele? Michele Cushatt?"

"Yes, it's me. Good to hear from you, Christine. How are you?" I tried not to sound disappointed.

"Oh." She hesitated. Sounding disappointed. "Actually, I was trying to call my friend Melissa. You're right next to her on my contact list. I must've hit your name by mistake."

Really, God? I need a friend, and this is all you can come up with?

"No problem." I moved to hang up.

She didn't. Instead, she threw a lifeline: "While I have you on the phone, do you mind if I pray for you?"

Silence hung thick between us. Pray? I fell to my knees.

"Yes. Yes, please. I'd love that."

I wish I had a transcript of that prayer, wish I could go back and savor each unsuspecting offering. Without knowing any of the events of the morning, Christine prayed for peace, for my heart and mind to be covered and secured by the presence of God, and that I would know, in no uncertain terms, God's overwhelming, incomparable love.

Amen.

Within a minute, maybe less, we said our goodbyes so Christine could call the friend she'd meant to call all along. Again I hung up the phone to an empty house. But this time, instead of hearing taunts of fear, I heard the whisper of God: *If I had sent anyone else, you would have called it a coincidence. I sent her, the one person you'd never expect, so you'd know it was me. I'm with you, Michele. I'm with you!*

That's all it took. I didn't start skipping through the house or planting daisies. Didn't sing hymns or quote long passages of memorized Scripture. But I did close wet eyes and say, "Thank you."

The day cancer showed up in my life, God showed up bigger. He served up a portion of his presence, enough for one day. Enough to reassure me I'm not alone.

He did the same a hundred times over in the days that followed.

~

I show love with food offerings.

Nearly every morning, I make my family a hot breakfast. Biscuits and gravy. Omelets and muffins. Waffles with fruit. After school, I serve up gooey chocolate-chip cookies and tall glasses of cold milk to my boys. When Troy's had a tough week at work, I put together a gourmet dinner with enough courses to earn a college degree.

It's what I do when I don't know what to do. I cook.

That's why, in spite of the diagnosis and unknowns, I still wanted to host Thanksgiving dinner. I couldn't eat, couldn't keep any food down because of the fear hijacking my stomach. Still, I cooked with a feverish desperation.

Guests began to arrive around noon: Don and Rhonda, dear friends and former neighbors whose two daughters had grown up with our boys; Damian, a college kid and friend of my oldest who'd been joining us for holiday dinners as long as I could remember; Troy's mom, Dana, who drove two hours to eat turkey with her grandchildren. These dear souls were more family members than friends, and they joined my parents, husband, and three boys to complete our Thanksgiving celebration. Honestly, I couldn't imagine anyone else I'd rather spend such a day with.

Soon, every inch of my kitchen reflected warmth, nourishment, and love: Steaming side dishes and chilled salads. A basket of homemade rolls served alongside a full stick of real butter. Cherry-red Jell-O with enough marshmallows and calories to ruin a faithful Weight Watcher in one serving. Creamy mashed potatoes whipped with an embarrassing amount of butter and half-and-half. Cinnamon-laced sweet potatoes. The best apple-walnut stuffing known to mankind. Gorgeous deep-dish pies—a gooey pecan, two cream-topped pumpkins, and a thick dark chocolate.

And towering above these lesser dishes, assuming one entire section of my granite-surfaced kitchen island, sat the glory of our feast: a golden-brown, twenty-two-pound turkey.

Cancer wasn't good for my peace. But it inspired quite a feast.

For me, the kitchen table has always been the axis around

which our family revolves. And the making of the food is how I keep our world spinning. There's something about feeding people that fills me with both peace and purpose. With my two hands, I create life-sustaining meals and serve them in generous, heaping portions to my family. And the satisfaction on their faces warms me from head to toe. In all the preparing and serving, I both love well and feel loved in return.

I prepare the plate; they eat it. And we both end up full.

I like to think God gets it. After all, he is the one who served up breakfast daily to his children. Manna from heaven. Sweet flakes falling from the sky.

Exodus 16 tells the story. For four hundred years, the Israelites had been slaves in Egypt, abused and mistreated by ruthless captors. So they cried and prayed, in fear and panic. And God showed up with a man called Moses to set them free. Overjoyed, they left Egypt behind in the hope of finding a Promised Land.

But they didn't expect to first endure a wilderness. The shine of the promise faded at the first pangs of hunger. Forgetting their rescue and the God who arranged it, they chose to whine in despair rather than revel in their freedom. How quickly one miracle is forgotten when another is wanted.

Even so, God promised to nourish: "I will rain down bread from heaven for you."[1]

Dinner dropped from the sky. Manna.

One condition, God warned: Gather only enough for today. I'll provide more tomorrow.

But hunger drives desperate behavior. The Israelites didn't listen. Instead, they pulled out the Tupperware. And those who stockpiled enough for the week ended up with stinking, maggot-infested leftovers.

Though I wish it weren't true, I'm no different. One-day-at-a-time living is difficult for me. I prefer to plot and plan, save and stock up. I gather and hoard for my unexpected tomorrows as if the Promised Land hinges on me. *On me.* But in my wilderness, my stockpiles turn rotten and unfulfilling. What can a full pantry and bulging 401(k) do for the woman facing cancer?

I will rain down bread from heaven for you.

He whispers it to me, again and again. Provision. But provision delivered in portions. One serving at a time. One day at a time. No stockpiles or truckloads. Not enough to fill a pantry, but certainly enough to fill a plate.

Can you trust me? he asks.

I couldn't answer that question on Thanksgiving Day. With a single phone call two days before, infinite life turned finite. A PET scan and more doctors' appointments loomed, during which doctors would stage the cancer's progression and provide me with as close to a definitive prognosis as the medical community can. Until then, even as I whipped up potatoes and gravy, I hovered in horrific limbo. Life and death wrestled at alternate poles with me in the middle, curled up in the fetal position. I needed to know I'd beat this to again sit at the Thanksgiving table the next year. But no one could make that promise. No one could tell me, for certain, that it would all turn out okay.

So while my family and guests ate platefuls of turkey and stuffing, I sneaked off to my bedroom, where I curled up on my bed, alone, and cried.

I'm afraid! I don't want to die, don't want to miss out on life.

But as it turns out, I did exactly that. Like Israelites consumed with hunger pangs, I couldn't see beyond the ache of my circumstances. Downstairs, a dozen of my dearest family and friends filled my dining room, laughing and celebrating the gift of life. But rather than savor the day with gratitude, I wanted a stockpile of reassurance about tomorrow. In my fear of death, I almost missed life.

It was my husband who finally helped me back to the feast. Finding me closed in behind bedroom doors, he wrapped sure arms around me.

"You okay?"

He didn't wait for an answer. Just held me close. Let me cry. Rubbed soft, tender circles on my back. Listened to my panicked questions without trying to fill the void with promises he couldn't make.

It was enough. Not for weeks and months to follow. But enough for that day. Enough to get me back to the table.

CHAPTER 3

Waiting

Jesus, say the word.
I am the bleeding woman.
The crippled woman.
The Samaritan woman.
The little girl.
I need your touch and your healing.
Extend my life . . . I want to live!

—JOURNAL ENTRY, November 29

I DON'T WAIT WELL.

I like answers, tangibles, plans. Not unknowns and waiting.

When I was eight and a half months pregnant with my youngest, Jacob, I was convinced I'd be pregnant until Jesus came in glory. Have mercy. At each weekly appointment, the doctor shook her head, both at my girth and the stubbornness of my unborn child. The baby wasn't going anywhere anytime soon. He seemed quite content eating at my internal buffet. So I heaved my enormous self home, where I whined and tried every birth-inducing remedy known to womankind, including three-mile waddles around the neighborhood and spicy food. As if.

In the end, it took a scheduled induction, gallons of IV

pitocin, and almost twenty-four hours of horrible labor to drag my reluctant nine-pound, five-ounce man-child into his life.

The Monday after Thanksgiving, the PET imaging clinic called to schedule my scan. I'd been waiting for their call for days, hovering near the phone like a girl desperate for a date.

We'd done the biopsy, had a preliminary appointment and physical exam with the surgeon, Dr. Forrester, to discuss the process and options. But none of us yet knew the extent of the disease. The biopsied ulcer had been giving me fits off and on for two to three years, at least. When had it turned cancerous? Last week? Last month? Last year? Had cancer cells been slithering through my body all that time, sabotaging healthy cells without my knowing it? The PET scan would tell the truth, for better or worse. Once the results were in, my doctor would know what we were working with, "stage" it, and set a plan to tackle it. Until then, I fretted and paced.

I took the first available appointment. December 1. Two days away. I hadn't slept well for a week, couldn't eat or function. I spent most days in a nervous panic. The thought of waiting two more days for my scan, followed by another four or five for results, made me want to throw up. Each twenty-four-hour block felt as taxing as a marathon. I was exhausted. But there was nothing I could do, no way around the waiting. In time, I'd learn the waiting is as much a part of the cancer journey as the scans and appointments.

The day of my PET scan arrived and I exhaled. Simply having something to do felt better than sitting at home waiting for answers. After arriving at the clinic and checking in, I was greeted by a tech who took me to a side room for a quick debriefing. PET stands for positron emission tomography. To begin, I'd receive an injection of a radioactive glucose, a tracer. The tracer would then travel to areas of the body with a higher metabolic rate—cancer cells—which is why people often claim cancer likes sugar. (Who knew we'd have something in common?) After the injection, I'd sit in a dark, quiet room for one hour while the clear liquid traveled through my veins, gathering anywhere cancer cells were having a picnic. Then, after the hour of waiting, waiting, waiting, I'd be taken to the scanning room, where I'd lie long and flat in a narrow, hollowed-out white tube. For those who panic at the thought of tight spaces, I wouldn't recommend it. For twenty-five minutes, I'd lie completely still, mummified by the white tube, while the technician took pictures of my body, head to midthigh. If cancer lurked, radioactive glucose would light up affected areas like a Christmas tree.

Happy Holidays to me.

Days before, my childhood friend Tangie sent me a text. She was having a long, painful dental procedure and felt more than a little apprehensive about it. The dentist planned to cut the gums away from her teeth to remove a granuloma. The thought of the pain terrified her (and me). We texted back and forth, and I did my best to give an encouraging pep talk and promised to pray. Later, when the procedure was over, she texted with news that the procedure ended up far more complicated than anticipated. "They were unable to numb my mouth after several attempts," she said. "I could feel everything he was doing." I couldn't imagine her pain and fear, how she endured. "I sang hymns in my head," she told me. "It got me through."

So as I lay inside the giant PET tube and a tech took images of my body, I thought of Tangie. And I sang hymns. Not out loud. But my heart sang, repeating words of the sacred songs I'd known by heart since I was a little girl.

O Lord my God, when I in awesome wonder
Consider all the worlds thy hands have made,
I see the stars, I hear the rolling thunder,
Thy power throughout the universe displayed:
Then sings my soul, my Savior God, to thee:
How great thou art! How great thou art![2]

"Great Is Thy Faithfulness." "Jesus, Lover of My Soul." "How Great Thou Art." Lyric after lyric, I allowed the familiarity of these sweet old hymns to cradle me in peace while the PET scan determined my fate.

In the process, I corrected my theology.

A PET scan doesn't determine the days of my life. The Great Thou Art does.

~

The peace I felt on the day of my PET scan disappeared by the time I woke up the following morning.

Fear swallowed all the truths that had reassured the day before. Again I waited for the phone to ring. I knew results could take days, but I paced and hovered, willing the answers to come. Waiting. Forever waiting.

Once again I retreated to my bedroom closet, a six-by-eight-foot area that had quickly become sacred space. I don't know how many times I fell on my face that day and week, but again and again I put forehead to carpet and pleaded with a delivering God: *I want to live!*

Emboldened by my desperation, I prayed big, ridiculous prayers, prayers that didn't make sense in a medical world of black-and-white facts. But I prayed them just the same, shaping my requests around specific results, using words like "no evidence of cancer" and "no sign that it was ever there." It seemed too much to ask, too big of a request. Especially considering the number of years the ulcer had lingered. But I had nothing to lose. If I truly believed in a real and powerful God, I'd better act like it now.

But my head knowledge had a hard time keeping up with my humanity. I'd leave my prayer closet with renewed determination to face this challenge with the courage and faith I'd claimed since I was seven years old. Sometimes the peace would last for an hour or two.

I trust you, God.

And I did. But then I'd receive a prayer request about a friend's horrific chemo treatments. Or I'd see a Facebook status about someone's new diagnosis. The truth about how many people—faithful, honest, trusting people—live with and die of cancer every day shook me. The worst *can* happen. There are no guarantees.

Soon the fear returned and my heart failed. *What if this is the beginning of the end? What if my boys have to grow up without me?*

Terrified, I'd crawl back to my closet and plant my face on the floor.

Help me!

In and out of that closet. Courageous one moment, terrified the next. Always, always, regardless of brief respites, by the time the sun set the fear consumed my insides like the heavy dark outside. Nighttime caused the beast to grow.

I suppose I should have anticipated such a reaction. This wasn't a the-dishwasher-stopped-working crisis. It was big, life altering. My family and future were at stake. Even so I expected more from myself. For four years I'd been a writer and speaker who encouraged audiences to live firmly rooted in the reality of

God. In fact, two days following my PET scan, I was scheduled to be the keynote speaker at a women's Christmas event. As I made worried tracks in the carpet, I chastised myself for my hypocrisy. I preached a good word on faith, challenged men and women to stand on their belief. But now, when life hiccupped—albeit a big hiccup—I couldn't seem to grasp my own message. How would I speak a hope- and peace-filled message to a room full of women when I couldn't find a scrap of either for myself?

Another long fear-filled day passed. As I headed to bed, exhausted but unsettled, I went to check email one last time before shutting my computer down. In the dark, with only the glare of my screen giving any light, I clicked open my inbox.

A message waited. From my doctor.

In an instant, my heart rate doubled and hands shook. *This is it.* I braced myself, clicked open the email, and read her message: "The PET scan did not pick up any cancer in your neck or elsewhere. In fact, the residual cancer in your tongue is so small that they couldn't see that either. I believe that is very good news regarding your overall prognosis with this! See you next week for surgery."

I fell to the floor.

Relief. Complete, draining relief.

Thank you. Thank you. Thank you.

Through an ocean of tears, I prayed the same two words over and over. It was all I could think to say. After days of verbose pleas and strategically quoted Psalms, I could hardly speak.

I read Dr. Forrester's words again, relishing each one. The journey ahead wouldn't be easy. I knew that. A major surgery, several weeks of painful recovery, and countless appointments that would last for at least five years. But the weight of a worst-case scenario lifted.

That's when I started dancing. I twirled through my house like a carefree five-year-old, telling my husband and children the good news. In between poorly executed dance moves, I here and there fell to my knees to give thanks again. I had no idea how much I loved my life, until I almost lost it.

In the middle of my gratitude-fest, it occurred to me I needed to do one more thing. I got back on my computer, pulled up my messages, and typed a reply to my new best friend and doctor: "I've been crying huge tears of relief over here all night long! Thank you so much for this wonderful news! I don't know what your beliefs are, but I believe with all my heart in Jesus. At least forty people (not to mention me and my own family!) have been praying their hearts out for the last week and a half. Though it seemed such a bold request, this is exactly what we were praying for. God is good. Much to be thankful for tonight."

I knew I probably sounded silly and ridiculous. But I didn't care. I wanted the world to know I believed in a God who could answer bold, ridiculous prayers in bold, ridiculous ways.

She wrote back quickly, probably laughing at my online evangelism. But her tempered reply sobered my enthusiasm just a bit: "Yes, God is good—I believe this even when we struggle to understand all of his purposes."

Her words stopped my twirling. It occurred to me then that she'd had to deliver bad news more than once. Not this time, thank heavens, but too many times before. How does a doctor make sense of the sparing of one life and the losing of another?

Yes. God is good. It was easy for me to say it at that moment, buoyed as I was with good test results. But would I still have celebrated the goodness of God with different results? Would I have testified to my confident, unwavering belief in Jesus had the PET scan turned out differently? I would like to think so. But honestly, I don't know.

That night I danced. I celebrated a God who heard my closet pleas and fought for the life of his child. I poured out gratitude like an offering. But later, when other prayers didn't receive such neat and tidy answers, I'd have to learn a different kind of dancing, the kind that stands still. The kind that leans into the sure arms of a mysterious and unfathomable God and allows him to lead, even when she doesn't know where he is leading.

Because sometimes God fights for his girl in ways she never imagined.

CHAPTER 4

A Cancer Far Worse

How can the inner workings of the heart be changed from a dynamic of fear and anger to that of love, joy and gratitude? Here is how. You need to be moved by the sight of what it cost to bring you home.

—TIMOTHY KELLER, *The Prodigal God*

THERE'S A STORY IN THE BIBLE ABOUT A FATHER AND HIS TWO sons.[3]

The older, a model of near perfection. The younger, impulsive and selfish. We hear little about the older brother, but the younger creates enough drama for twenty-two verses. Hungry for the rush of indulgence and popularity, he demands his inheritance from his still-living father. He wants to party and believes cash is the key to his happiness. The father, knowing that some lessons can be learned only the hard way, gives his son what he asks. And, filled with grief, he lets him go.

For a while, the son lives it up. He indulges in his freedom, spends lavishly without thought or care. This is what he wanted, what he'd been missing! But soon reality tarnishes the dream. The money runs out. The friends run off. And a famine, both literal and figurative, leaves him with nothing. Starving and with nowhere left to go, the younger son heads home. To his father.

The entire story hinges on a single moment, a split second in a plot stretched with tension. The son approaches his father's home, broke and broken. The father, having endured the ache of a lost child too long, squints at the familiar form in the distance. *Can it be?* For the briefest moment, son looks at father and father looks at son. What will the father do? Send the ungrateful, foolish child away? Or welcome him home?

"But the father said to his servants, 'Quick! Bring the best robe and put it on him. Put a ring on his finger and sandals on his feet. Bring the fattened calf and kill it. Let's have a feast and celebrate. For this son of mine was dead and is alive again; he was lost and is found.'"[4]

Dead, then alive! Lost, then found!

The moment my doctor delivered those beautiful, glorious PET scan results, I resurrected. For weeks I'd been dead in the waiting and worrying and unknowns. Broke and broken. Limping and empty. Now, with her words—"no evidence of disease"—the lost girl found her way back home.

I was no longer dying; I was living.

If I'd had a fattened calf, I would've grilled it faster than you can say "filet mignon."

It's a horrible thing to think you've lost your life. But it's a wonderful thing to find it again. I hadn't realized how much I valued my breath until I thought it might end. With renewed hope, I wanted to savor every moment, every morsel this life can offer.

A celebration. That's what we needed. So Troy planned a date, a full afternoon and evening of doing ordinary things together. Christmas shopping for the boys, dinner at a nice restaurant, and two tickets to *The Nutcracker* ballet in downtown Denver. Our own fattened calf.

But, like everything else that month, the date didn't go according to plan.

It started fine, with a quick lunch and shopping. In less than two hours we got half our Christmas shopping done. Filled to bursting with gratitude, I bought a little of everything for my boys. Movies, games, their favorite chocolates and bubble gum. After paying for our purchases, we loaded up our bags and headed back to the parking lot. Troy may have walked, but I nearly skipped the entire way to his truck. More stores and shopping awaited us, and I was enjoying every bite of this slice of ordinary life.

Merry Christmas!

That's when I saw the window. Rather, the empty space where the window used to be.

Glass shards littered the cement at my feet. It took a full minute for my mind to recognize what my eyes took in: while we shopped, a thief had broken into our truck.

Over the next few minutes, we catalogued all we'd lost. Christmas gifts already purchased. Gift cards. The GPS. A Kindle. Troy's wallet. (Yes, he left it behind.) Every item of value had been stolen.

Wait.

I blinked, shook my head. Not true. Everything I valued I still had.

My husband, whose calming presence and wisdom had become a bulwark to me over the past weeks. My boys, who daily reminded me of what it feels like to love someone more than yourself. And this mysterious and unfathomable God and Father who, though I could not always understand him, had become more real to me than ever before.

No, a vandal couldn't take what I had. The best of my life was still intact.

There was a time when a thief could've robbed me of that day's celebration. I would've kicked the tire or screamed in frustration. But this time, with life and death as the backdrop, the injustice hardly registered. As my friend Becky later reminded me, "If you can write a check for it, it isn't a tragedy."

Ah, yes. Truth.

Troy called the police, while I called insurance and credit card companies. Over the next hour, we filed a report, canceled cards, and scheduled a repair. By the time we got the logistics taken care of, we didn't have time to finish shopping before the ballet began. We barely had time to drive home, exchange cars, and grab a quick dinner.

So we readjusted. Like we had so many times over the preceding weeks. We took a deep breath, embraced our new reality, and enjoyed a beautiful *Nutcracker* ballet.

Not an ideal date. But a wonderful one.

And just like that, we forgave the offense of a nameless vandal.

~

Almost exactly four years before that night, long before my health crisis showed up and a thief vandalized our truck, I watched a cancer steal the life of our church.

We'd been there fifteen years, from the week it began as a church plant in an elementary school, through exponential growth, a building campaign, and a new facility. We knew nearly every member by name, had watched each other's children grow up. We'd taught Sunday school classes, volunteered in the youth group, and led worship. Our church was both home and family. We loved it.

Which is why watching it die tore me in two. I felt like a child caught in the middle of her parents' nasty divorce.

The details of what happened and why aren't important. I'm sure some remember it differently than I do. It's enough to say that pride, selfish ambition, and emotions got the better of a couple of key groups of people. What followed over the course of months was a poisonous dividing, a splitting into hostile camps. One group advocated for this. Another advocated for that. Fervent about their reasons, fueled by tender wounds and a sense of justification, both sides fought for their positions.

The cancer culminated late one Sunday night in a church auditorium thick with tension. A congregational meeting, they called it. A gathering of my dearest friends. Leaders hurled words like weapons. Congregants bared emotions like fangs. Within the conflict, several fought for peace and calm, pleaded for a biblical solution. But emotion drowned out reason.

I wept that night, knowing there would be no winners. While conflict ensued in the auditorium, I exited the double doors and dropped to my knees in the carpeted hall: *God, save us! Do something!*

Somehow, hours from closing its doors, our church managed to survive both that congregational meeting and the cancer. Hundreds exited, leaving a broken few to try to fix the mess. It took years for a measure of healing to come. Even then, the church we'd loved for so long never stopped walking with a limp.

Nor did I. The whole situation devastated me. I'd grown up in a strong, healthy church. Not perfect, but good. The richness of that Christian community set a standard I'd spent my adult years searching for. To see it fall so far from its potential and purpose grieved me. And changed me. I was angry with leadership who could allow it to happen, disappointed with those who'd allowed both pride and position to become tumors more consuming than grace.

We remained at that church for another five years. Licking wounds and limping, along with everyone else who stuck around. But we weren't the same. None of us were the same.

I lost my innocence the year our church split, the tender, trusting part of me who grew up seeing God's church as a haven, a family.

It certainly can be. But not when God's people allow disease to spread unchecked.

I wasn't sure I'd ever be able to absolve the vandals of that.

~

Friday, December 10. Surgery day. A partial glossectomy, that's what Dr. Forrester called it. The biopsy had confirmed cancerous cells. Now they needed to remove a larger section of tissue to ensure clean margins around the affected area.

In less glamorous terms, she was going to cut out part of my tongue. Like a gnarly scene from a pirate movie. Not something a mom of three adds to her Google calendar. Let's just say I was feeling some separation anxiety. My tongue and I had grown rather attached.

Sure, we celebrated the night of the *Nutcracker*, enjoyed every bite of our fattened calf. But I was naive to believe my post-PET-scan high would last through the tension of surgery week. It didn't. As December 10 moved closer, the peace of the prior Friday ebbed as fear of the next Friday grew.

The surgery would last an hour, Dr. Forrester said. If recovery went well, I'd be home later that afternoon. For at least two weeks, I'd "eat" liquids, then baby-soft foods: applesauce, pudding, runny mashed potatoes. Talking would be nonexistent for the first few days, limited for several weeks following. This, I'm quite sure, my husband celebrated. I, not so much. I feared weeks of biting my tongue (so to speak) would cause me to swell with unexpressed words and explode like a Gallagher watermelon.

A mess, I tell you.

In all seriousness, the aftereffects of such a surgery terrified me. I worried about things like how I would breathe with all the swelling. How I'd eat, drink, and swallow. Not to mention the brutal pain. What would I do when the nausea and vomiting hit? The thought of throwing up did not thrill me.

Monday. Tuesday. Ever closer inched Friday. Unable to eat because of my anxiety and pain, I'd lost close to fifteen pounds in a month. Worse yet, I couldn't sleep without sleeping pills. Even then, I often lay awake through the night, cataloguing scenes from my too-short thirty-nine years.

Those lazy childhood fishing trips to Minnesota with my parents.

Our day-after-Thanksgiving treks to cut down the perfect Christmas tree.

Dancing with Troy on our wedding day.

Bedtime tuck-ins and lullaby-singing with my boys.

I stared at the bedroom ceiling and envied my husband's rhythmic breathing. Reliving those key moments didn't bring comfort like I thought it would. I treasured them, yes. But I also mourned how I'd squandered them. In all my rush to make the next memory and snap the next photo, I'd missed the significance. Flippant. I'd been flippant about far too much.

I awoke Thursday morning a zombie, bleary eyed and dragging

my half-dead self from room to room. A bit overly dramatic, but fear does that. It puts a magnifying glass on a gnat and shows it as a Goliath.

Panicked by my Goliath, I started more negotiations with God.

Help me, God. Do something, anything. I can't keep going this way.

This time he replied. Not audibly and not how I expected. But his presence and words came in an Elijah-like whisper of glory I could not mistake: *You're so worried about this cancer, Michele. Consumed over whether it will eat away your life. But you have a cancer far worse in your heart.*

What? I do?

Unforgiveness. You need to let it go.

God's rebuke shushed me silent.

The grievances I'd long held against friends and family members. The countless times I'd lost it with my boys. My disappointment with my husband when he didn't listen or say what I needed him to say.

And my resentment toward those who nearly destroyed our church.

I'd been consumed by thoughts of surgery, pain, and metastasis all while continuing to nurse wounds and wrongs I hadn't made right.

Cancer. And I needed to cut it out.

Forgiveness, of the authentic and true kind, is a rare find. We spend years restoring worn antiques, hundreds of dollars repairing wrecked and dented cars. But if a relationship sustains damage, we're more likely to relegate it to the scrap heap than try to restore its shine. We're far more enduring with our valuables than with the people we claim to value. As a result, we accumulate junkyards filled with harsh words, hurt feelings, and damaged relationships. We toss people to the side, punish them for their fallibility. But eventually the wreckage grows beyond our ability to disguise.

It's foolish, really, how I believed my unforgiveness caused the offending party a measure of my pain. But cancer threatens only the one carrying it.

In a moment, urgency replaced anxiety. Now that I was faced with death, the injustices that once seemed important showed themselves to be trivial. And the grudges that seemed inconsequential showed themselves to be nearly cancerous.

Time to let the vandals go.

Less than twenty-four hours before surgery, I pulled out my scalpel and made phone calls, wrote emails, and initiated difficult conversations. With friends, former friends, and family members. Uncomfortable? Yes. A cutting out of the unforgiveness to which I'd grown attached. To this day it remains some of the hardest work I've ever done. But by the end of the last "I'm sorry" and "Will you forgive me?" a weight lifted. Nothing remained unfinished.

Peace.

The day before surgery, I begged God to relieve my fear. Instead, he relieved a weight far heavier: unforgiveness.

Like both the foolish son in the distance and the grieving father on the front porch, the story hinged on one split-second decision.

Reject or receive? Refuse or restore?

And for the grace of the Father who'd done the same for me, I chose life over death. Forgiveness over fear. For both myself and those who'd failed me.

And found my way home.

CHAPTER 5

Till Death Do Us Part

Time is
Too slow for those who wait,
Too swift for those who fear,
Too long for those who grieve,
Too short for those who rejoice.
But for those who love,
Time is eternity.
Hours fly, flowers die,
New days, new ways pass by,
Love stays.

—HENRY VAN DYKE
(in Sarah McElwain, *Saying Grace*)

I LOVE ANESTHESIA MORE THAN DESSERT.

No, really.

I slipped into surgical unconsciousness like a baby in a warm bath, too drugged and warm and soft to feel the least bit embarrassed about my scantily clad self. Bliss, I tell you. Absolute bliss.

No, *really*. The last time I slept that well, I was floating in amniotic fluid.

Happy, oh so happy. For an hour or two.

And then I woke up. With a fat, mammoth tongue big enough to make me choke. And fully aware of my scantily clad self. In a moment, the sweet fog of ignorance disappeared and reality slapped me wide awake like a doctor's gloved hand on my backside.

I'd had surgery. For cancer.

Cotton filled my mouth. The nurse asked if I wanted ice chips and pain pills. I nodded, mouth and throat too sore to croak out a simple "Yes, please."

I needed Troy. Frantic, I searched the recovery room. IV poles. Other half-naked, unconscious patients. Nurses bustling, doctors conferring. But no sign of my husband.

For the next hour, I slipped in and out of sleep. At one point, the nurse handed me a paper cup filled with pills. I'm not sure how I choked them down, but it involved no small amount of drooling.

Again, sleep.

Minutes later—or was it hours?—the nurse had me dressed and sitting up in a chair, signing discharge forms I couldn't read. My eyeballs were still flying high in the happy swirly place of anesthesia heaven.

And then he came. Troy. Close enough to touch. Tender, concerned. Holding my hand.

I don't think handholding ever felt as good as it did that day. His hand swallowed my smaller one in its strength. However lost I'd felt before he showed up, I found myself in his grasp. I knew he had me. Regardless of what the next days and weeks of recovery looked like, he wouldn't let me go. I gripped his hand like the human lifeline it was.

Within minutes, the nurse pulled up with a wheelchair and helped me in. I'd normally refuse this embarrassing sign of weakness. The surgery had been on my mouth, not my legs. I could walk.

Only I couldn't. I had noodles for legs, a cannonball for a head. Troy lifted me like a doll, and I melted into the rolling chair. And both the nurse and my husband wheeled me to the front doors. There my parents waited with the same look of concern and worry I'd seen in Troy's eyes. They tried to mask it, show only cheer and positivity. It was a good thing. I needed hopeful faces. I'd felt enough fear for all of us.

By midafternoon, we were on our way home through the streets of downtown Denver and toward the quiet of suburbia. I slept most of the way, occasionally nudged awake by the feel of Troy's hand reaching over to grab mine, his thumb rubbing reassuring circles on my skin.

Halfway between the hospital and home, in a brief waking moment, a single thought poked through my fog like the sun's rays through a cloud.

We almost didn't make it, Troy and I. Our marriage had been a gamble against the odds. From the first day, an impossible endeavor. Every day since, it had demanded more sweat and tears than I could've imagined.

I squeezed my husband's hand.

Unable to speak, but determined to hold on.

~

I was the pastor's wife before I was Troy's wife.

Twenty-one years old and living the dream.

I must've been in middle school when I started praying for my one-day husband. Whether it was the result of a Sunday sermon or the guidance of my God-loving parents, I believed praying for a husband was the surest way to hit the fairytale-family jackpot. That and going to a Christian college. So I prayed until I was eighteen, and then went to Christian college. The Christian girl's foolproof plan to land the perfect life.

I met him my first week on campus. I a freshman and missions major. He a junior in music ministry. During a school-sponsored event, I found myself watching a Disney movie under a canopy of stars with this six-foot-two, talk-dark-and-handsome upperclassman.

Holy happily-ever-after. I'd hit the jackpot.

What followed over the next three years felt like a dream come true. A shared love of music, old movies, and classic books. A heart for ministry and a desire for a big family. A friendship and an on-again, off-again romance that culminated in a storybook wedding in front of hundreds of our closest friends and family. Idyllic. Perfect. Everything I'd spent a lifetime praying for.

It took less than a month for the mirage to fade.

I've long held this part of my story close to my chest. It's difficult, private, and I have a beautiful son whose light birthed out of that darkness. Besides, more than twenty years have passed. Time has, no doubt, altered my recollection of events. All I know is God worked a Lazarus-size healing, and I'm reticent to return to the tomb.

But I will say this. In the end, addiction destroyed my marriage. And I was too immature and disillusioned to know how to handle it. During that handful of years, I became a person I'd never wanted to become, drowning in anger, loneliness, and despair. Afraid to expose the darkness destroying our family, I isolated at home, alone. I cried more than I smiled, screamed and begged more than I talked. Even when I gave birth to a son, Jacob, hope remained out of reach. For no matter how hard I tried, no matter how worn my knees from pleading with God for deliverance, I could do nothing to save the marriage and man I loved.

Six days before Christmas and six years after our wedding, while holding my baby boy, I watched my pastor husband—and my dream—drive away for the last time.

When you are raised to believe in the covenant of marriage, few things devastate like the ripping of divorce. "God hates divorce" is a phrase I heard nearly as often as "God is love." But how was I to reconcile the two? Could God overlook his hatred of divorce to still love me? Could he see me beyond my scarlet *D*? I doubted it.

The judgments and stigma that seemed to follow such a breach didn't help. Overnight I'd become anathema, an example of what others wanted to avoid. Friends didn't know what to say, so they stayed away. Old college friends called to quote Scripture and save my wayward soul. Former family members treated me like I didn't exist. My previous value and potential appeared to be lost in my divorced and single-mom status.

To my relief, our church embraced us, allowed me and my son to stay long after my husband was gone. Like a long exhalation, I sank into the safety of that church family with gratitude. I needed a safe place to heal and learn how to be a single mother.

Still, shame followed me. How could I blame the judgers when I judged myself? Hadn't I committed the unpardonable? My evangelical upbringing raised me to believe, without question, in the permanency of marriage. "Till death do us part" stood as sacred as the Ten Commandments. I'd failed the most critical of callings.

It took me a decade to forgive myself and exchange the "divorced" label for a "grace" one. Almost ten years to learn that

God's love is indeed strong enough to redeem the heartbreak of divorce. Until then I mothered and worked with a desperation known only to those who believe they've failed their children in the worst way.

There, in the messy middle of my penance, I met Troy. A divorced, single dad of two small boys, three and five years older than my son. We attended the same small church plant in the southern suburbs of Denver, Colorado, and his story was as unwanted and devastating as mine. Two single parents in a congregation filled with traditional families.

We stood out like steaks on a vegetarian's table. The makings of a natural alliance.

It took more than a year of friendship to cross over into something resembling love. Even then our affection bloomed from a broken and lonely place more than from a whole and healthy one. I had no intention of dating or marrying again. I didn't want to get hurt again, and neither did he. In spite of myself, I began to again dream of a kitchen table filled with people. I imagined family vacations, baseball games, Christmas mornings, and bedtime tuck-ins. With a Prince Charming in place, I could resurrect my dream of happily-ever-after.

Two years after we met, we married in an outdoor ceremony overlooking the Rocky Mountains. With three little boys—four, seven, and nine—holding our hands.

"Now we're going to be a happy family," my nine-year-old stepson said on our wedding day. I loved that he held such hope for our family, and I believed him. But neither of us had any idea how difficult remarriage with children could be.

A "blended family," they call it, which I find laughable now. Five individuals thrown into a high-powered electrical kitchen appliance along with the frozen ruins of two divorces nobody wanted. And we think that's going to blend? Stepfamilies do not blend like peanuts into peanut butter or strawberries into smoothies. They blend like nails and screws. Regardless of high hopes and good intentions, there's a good chance someone's going to get hurt.

Which is what happened. To all of us.

The truth is we entered our family already broken. We all do, traditional families and stepfamilies alike. But more so the families that survive divorce and loss and attempt to heal themselves by creating new families.

The day of our wedding, the five of us showed up dressed in lace and pearls, slacks and ties. But behind the pressed and polished costumes, each one of us bled. Our divorces had ripped us in two, adults and children alike. We mourned even in our joy.

I knew the statistics, understood that the odds of success were not in our favor. But it took the real life after "I do" to help me understand why. Marriage is hard work, even without the added obstacles of stepfamilies. But add parenting schedules, split holidays, complicated relationships with exes, legal battles, and children caught between two opposing parenting styles, and you have quite a mess. And that was only the beginning.

The years of so-called blending weathered each of us—weathered me—like the cushions on my outdoor furniture. I was worn, frayed around the edges, covered with holes. Weary from the struggle and again disillusioned by marriage, I became a lesser version of myself. Negative. Dissatisfied.

This isn't what I signed up for, I remember thinking more than once. It was too hard, without enough good days to make up for the bad ones. Now I understood why second marriages often end in divorce. Faced with the impossibility of our task, I could see only the losses, the many ways our family and marriage didn't measure up to the dream. And I wanted the pain to stop.

It all came down to a choice. Not so much a single, profound moment of decision but a long slow revelation over months and years. I could not sit as a spectator to my marriage, warming a bleacher seat while criticizing the bad plays and bad calls. Complaining about the unfairness and failure. That would lead only to misery.

Instead, I needed to leave or cleave. To walk away or play ball.

I decided to stay. To invest. To try to become a better version of me, rather than a lesser one. For starters, I paid more attention to what was beautiful and good than to the handful of things that were wrong. I stopped voicing every frustration and dissatisfaction. Swallowing my negative commentary—both internal and external—I offered words of affirmation and encouragement. Rather than drag my marriage and stepfamily around like a plan-B obligation, I started to speak of them—and to believe it—as a gift. They had been a gift all along, of course. A miraculous redemption of too much loss. It just took me a few years to push through the pain and see them as such. The healing had to come before the receiving.

I had no idea that years later, when I was buried by the fear of cancer, the man and marriage I once feared were a mistake would become the relationship I needed.

~

I fell back in love with my husband the Christmas after cancer.

Those first days postsurgery passed in a nauseated, medicated blur. I don't remember much, but I remember how Troy kept a log of my medications, doses and times, to make sure I didn't overdose (both thoughtful and wise). How, in the middle of the night, he stumbled to the kitchen to get a cup of applesauce to ease my nausea (again thoughtful and wise). I remember the sign he taped to the door with "I love you!" written in fat red letters, and how he guarded me from well-intentioned guests who asked questions I couldn't answer.

"She can't talk," he reminded them, then shooed them out the door and me off to bed.

And I remember how, when the thoughts and pain tormented at the end of each day, he'd crawl under my covers and pull me close.

"Tell me again," I begged. "Tell me it's going to be alright."

"It's going to be okay, Michele. You're going to be fine." How many times did he say those words?

During those moments, when the fear choked and the tears flowed, I remembered how close I'd come to walking away. Like the panic that follows a near car accident, I shook with awareness. It could've turned out so differently.

It has been said, "A happy marriage is the union of two good forgivers." I now understand what this means, and how wise and true the words are. A marriage isn't made of lace and pearls, slacks and ties. Nor can it be polished to a perfect shine or wrestled into submission. But it can be built one "I'm sorry," "I forgive you," and "I love you" at a time.

Early in our relationship, Troy's uncommunicative, unemotional, stubborn self frustrated and wounded me. I wanted more from him, needed more. But as I faced the possibility of death, I started to see the flip side of his flaws: the loyalty that grew from his stubbornness; the unflinching faith that quieted his emotions; the peace his wordless presence provided. The same qualities I'd before resented—and that would likely irritate me again—made the bedrock that supported me as I learned to live again.

Author and philosopher Sam Keen said, "We come to love not by finding a perfect person, but by learning to see an imperfect person perfectly."[5] Yes, that's it exactly. Against all odds, Troy became the dream the middle-school girl had prayed for.

Prince Charming? No. Ten years of marriage had revealed the fairytale to be nothing but fluff. He was—is—real. Human, flawed, and quite infuriating at times. But he wasn't riding off into the sunset and leaving me to endure this alone. He was standing, loyal and true, right next to me.

Holding my hand.

Till death do us part.

CHAPTER 6

In Pursuit of Peace

I've wanted your nearness like air.
And, somehow . . . you have done this . . .
It is terrifying.
And wonderful.
. . . as if a fog has lifted and I see clearly for the first time . . .
The beauty and wonder in this place is almost more
than I can bear.
I'm overcome.

—JOURNAL ENTRY, December 27

I WAS FIVE YEARS OLD WHEN I DISCOVERED GOD IS REAL.

Not a real thought or idea. But a real person, as tangible as the worn and frayed stuffed kitty I clutched under my arm.

My memory begins well into the evening, after, no doubt, a burning Arizona sunset. A favorite aunt and uncle reclined on the teal-and-green-patterned sofa, one of the seventies' regretful productions. My toddler brother annoyed me from his perch on the shag carpet. I remember the adults' easy conversation and my thrill at being allowed to stay up and listen.

Until I heard the words no child wants to hear: "Michele, it's time for bed."

Banished. The horror! My oppressor—the man I called Daddy—couldn't have delivered a more devastating blow. In the span of a few words, I went from queen of the castle to cast-out pauper. To go to bed meant to miss out on the evening's fun. By morning, my aunt and uncle would be long gone. Thus I did what any child does in such a life-altering and utterly unfair situation.

I threw a fit.

Here's where my memory grows fuzzy. One moment my father ordered me to bed. The next I'm buried under the covers in my darkened bedroom, crying deep gut-splitting sobs. Only vague images sit in between, including a tantrum worthy of Scarlett O'Hara. I'm pretty sure I deserved an Oscar.

I didn't want to go to bed. But that's not the only reason I cried. I'd failed to say goodbye. In the drama birthed of my disappointment, I'd turned my back on my aunt and uncle and stomped to my room. There, alone, I felt nothing but regret.

That's when my five-year-old self prayed. Sunday school teachers had told me about the big God in heaven, how he listened and cared. How I could talk to him about anything at all. I believed them.

Dear God, help my aunt or uncle to come into my room. So I can say I'm sorry. And goodbye. Please, God. Please!

It was a child's prayer, simple and selfish. I didn't want to feel the pain in my chest anymore. Over and over, I said the same words, eyes squeezed, tears rolling. *Please, God, please!* As if I could will him to work out my grief with the fervency of my wish.

Then.

The door cracked and light from the hallway spilled into my room.

Framed by soft yellow, my uncle entered quietly. He walked to the side of my bed, knelt down.

"I'm sorry!" I threw my arms around his neck, the tears pouring out along with my words.

I don't remember him speaking. There's a pretty good chance I might have shocked him into silence. Nor do I think it matters. Within seconds, we hugged, I said my burning goodbye, and he was gone, back out the bedroom door to rejoin the conversation in the living room.

The hall light vanished, as did my grief. My room resumed the shade of night once again.

But I would never be the same.

God came. I called to him and, in spite of my bad behavior, he answered. In the form of a favorite uncle, God made sure I knew he had heard me.

Decades later, as I stretched out on the family room couch recovering from cancer surgery, unable to speak or swallow for the pain, I thought of how God accomplished far more in the heart of that five-year-old girl than a second chance at a goodbye. Although vast and unfathomable, he knew I needed to see him as real. Not some two-dimensional, flannel-board cutout. Not a God "up there" or "out there" and beyond my reach. Not a God reserved for Sunday school teachers and sweet picture books.

A God for me. *With me.* Close enough to touch. Always listening, always working. He knew a day would come when I'd need more than cliches and anecdotes, more than cute stories and neatly packaged feelings.

And so he gave me himself. In a powerful, memory-searing way to the five-year-old girl crying tears on her pillow.

But belief wasn't always that easy. Real life turned out to be far more complicated than a girl forgetting to say goodbye to a favorite uncle. Prayers didn't always get answered the right way. Sometimes it seemed God stayed far away. From my perch on the couch, I didn't blame God for cancer. I didn't feel bitter, angry, or unjustly treated. I just felt confused. Hadn't I done everything right? I'd eaten healthy, taken care of myself, avoided tobacco. I exercised five or six days a week, slept eight hours a night. Heck, I flossed. Daily. That deserved bonus points.

I wonder if this is how the disciples felt in those tension-filled days after Jesus' death. They'd banked their entire lives and families on Jesus being real, the true Son of God. They'd seen him turn water into wine, heal the sick, even raise the dead back to life.

But they'd also seen stakes driven into his hands and a sword thrust into his side. Those who stuck around, who didn't flee in fear and panic, watched his final exhalation, listened to the wails of his mother as she mourned. He rescued and resurrected countless others. Couldn't he have done the same for himself? For them? And if he could have, why didn't he?

Were they bitter? Not that I can tell. Confused? Yes. And heartbroken.

In the absence of understanding, the disciples, the ones who'd seen Jesus work the miraculous day after day, panicked and ran. Their king was now a criminal. Because they'd cavorted with an enemy of the state, their lives were in danger. So they split, holed up in a room together with doors locked and knees knocking.

Had Jesus been nothing more than a mirage? Had they believed and followed a sham? They hadn't expected the story to turn out as it did.

Then light spilled from the hallway.

"On the evening of that first day of the week, when the disciples were together, with the doors locked for fear of the Jewish leaders, Jesus came and stood among them."[6]

Jesus, alive? Impossible. They blinked and fanned their faces. A wish? Or real?

"'Peace be with you!'"

The mirage spoke. The first words of the Savior to the saved.

"The disciples were overjoyed when they saw the Lord. Again Jesus said, 'Peace be with you!'"[7]

All it took was the presence of Jesus for terror and tension to flee. Not a change in circumstances or a reassurance of how the rest of the story would play out. Not even a solid answer to the question of why.

Instead, presence.

Peace isn't a byproduct of control, the payout of a happy conclusion. Peace is the infiltrating, life-giving presence of a very real God. One who loves nothing more than to step into the middle of locked and darkened rooms and impossible circumstances, close enough to touch.

It took me half a lifetime to learn this lesson, to see my need for presence over perfection. From the beginning, my fantasy of a perfect life was just that—a fantasy. It grew from the innocent and untried imagination of a girl who wanted her life to read like a fairytale.

But I'd forgotten that even fairytales have villains and hardships and unexpected twists in plot. I kept holding out for my happy ending, but missed the fact that I'd already received it.

A hero who pushed past my fear with the reassurance of his very real presence.

"Peace be with you!" he said. He still says.

To the five-year-old crying tears on her pillow, and to the grown-up woman who needed his touch from her place on the family room couch.

~

The organ pipes, one hundred and eight of them, reached like large golden arms toward heaven. Every eye in the church's sanctuary, including my own, turned upward. We couldn't help ourselves.

Christmas Eve. Fourteen days postsurgery. Earlier that night, I ate soft food that didn't require a blender or a straw. I showered, put on makeup, and dressed in my holiday finest. By 11:00 p.m., I sat in a long wooden pew, three quarters of the way back on the left side, sandwiched between my husband and three sons. There was no other place on earth I wanted to be.

I saw the organist's shoulders widen and lift as he breathed deeply and prepared to play. Raising both hands and head, he began to dance on white keys and dark, wooden pedals, arms and feet moving in perfect camaraderie. Like wise men from the East, the organist offered his gift to a newborn king. In the process, he delivered a slice of heaven to those of us looking up from earth.

O holy night, the stars are brightly shining;
It is the night of the dear Savior's birth!

I closed my eyes and allowed the organist and his pipes to both serenade and soothe. The music, long a language I knew and understood, washed over me, cleansing me of weeks of tension. Muscles released, stomach settled.

Every Christmas Eve, regardless of circumstance or weather, we play hooky from our home church. Instead, a couple of hours before midnight, we drive the forty minutes from our suburban home to an old stone church in downtown Denver. In a room of strangers, lifted by the music of a single organist and the voices of a hundred worshipers, we celebrate Jesus' birth along with the centuries: "Glory to God in the highest! And, on earth, peace."[8]

Founded in 1865, Trinity United Methodist is Denver's oldest church. The building, completed December 1888, oozes history. Rhyolite and sandstone decorate the outside. Inside, the posts and rails are constructed of carved oak. Stained-glass windows give the room both color and natural light.

As for Trinity's Roosevelt pipe organ (No. 380), the wonder extends far beyond the obvious. Behind the one hundred eight pipes visible from the pews sit four thousand ninety-four others, varying in length from one inch to thirty-two feet and constructed of everything from mahogany and pine to zinc and tin. It's an intricate structure, hidden away from public view. But when the dancing hands of the organist take their position, music explodes for all to hear.

Surrounded by such history, I thought of the thousands of parishioners who likewise celebrated Jesus' birth on the same wooden pews: mothers and fathers, sons and daughters, husbands and wives. Those who held hammer and nail to build the sanctuary in which I now sat were no longer. Those who'd take my seat decades from now were, perhaps, not yet born. But for this day, this year, the seat was mine. I felt the wood, strong against my back. Felt the floor, solid and unyielding.

Gooseflesh covered my arms and legs. Alive. I was alive!

> *A thrill of hope, the weary soul rejoices,*
> *For yonder breaks a new and glorious morn.*

I'd been given a second chance at life. The opportunity to live better, love more. I wanted to slow the service, hold each moment like a jewel in my hand, turn over the sights and sounds and marvel at the sparkle and shine. Facing the reality of death does this to a person. It transforms the routine into something of the miraculous. It turns handholding into a moment of magic. An organist's music into the songs of angels. The faces of your children into the makings of history.

The choir director led the singers through well-rehearsed songs. The pastor presented an inspired message of God's love for mankind. Soloists stood on the balcony, a cappella voices echoing off the hardwoods—choir loft, balusters, and pews—giving the entire presentation a depth of holiness. Gloved musicians rang their handbells, working in perfect harmony, one person and one note at a time, to create a symphony of music possible only with the uniting of many hands.

I sat in my pew, overcome. Like light spilling into a darkened room, an awareness of God's nearness filled me. It was as if he opened my eyes and ears to see the world—my life—from the vantage point of timelessness. In that moment, beyond all explanation, the fog of circumstance lifted. Everything became clear.

My life was merely one detail in a beautifully crafted story that opened at the dawning of time. Cancer, although wretched and worthy of grief, wasn't the defining characteristic of my life. Or anyone else's life. It was merely scenery in a vast and glorious story.

God created. God blessed. God rejected. God mourned. God promised. God loved. God gave. God healed. God rescued. God redeemed. God will come again!

Fall on your knees, O hear the angel voices!
O night divine, O night when Christ was born!
O night, O holy night, O night divine!

As I sat in a pew with hundreds of others, I could see the timeline of my life from the sight line of eternity. I'd been so desperate for assurances of health and longevity. I wanted answers and specifics. Cancer, in all its erratic unpredictability, had left me exposed, vulnerable, and afraid.

But with golden pipes lifting my eyes toward heaven, I sank into safety. It was a rare moment of clarity and focus, one that I later recalled and leaned against when the euphoria faded into the hundreds of tough days that followed. It wasn't something I expected or orchestrated, but like a kiss on the cheek, it landed soft and gentle, warming me head to toe. I knew if I reached for it, tried to grasp it in my hand, the moment would fly away. So I held my breath, closed my eyes, and released myself to the revelation.

For a brief moment, I knew to my bones that God would never let me go. Like four thousand pipes hidden behind one hundred others, he'd been working in the invisible realm, making all the parts and pieces fit together in a plan I couldn't fathom. God, real and close enough to touch, had been dancing on the keys of my life, childhood to adulthood, making music I couldn't fully understand.

> *Led by the light of faith serenely beaming,*
> *With glowing hearts by His cradle we stand.*
> *He knows our need—to our weakness is no stranger.*
> *Behold your King; before Him lowly bend!*[9]

After more than a month of fear, peace descended, for a time. Isaiah had prophesied the coming of the one. "Wonderful Counselor, Mighty God, Everlasting Father," Isaiah called him. But he saved the best name for last, the one that meant the most to me: "Prince of Peace."[10]

The pastor called us forward, row by row of men and women and children, to receive communion. I lowered myself to the kneeling rail, feeling small, shy even. I brought my palms together and opened them like a cup.

"The body of Christ, broken for you." She put the wafer in my hands, a gift I couldn't reach for and grab. I could only open myself to receive.

"The blood of Christ, shed for you." She held the goblet, filled with the rich burgundy of wine. I plunged my wafer into its depths, submerging it fully before lifting it to my lips.

"Peace I leave with you," Jesus would eventually say, when childhood gave way to manhood and a painful walk to a cross. "Do not let your hearts be troubled and do not be afraid."[11]

Okay, I get it. You are my peace.

Peace wasn't a feeling or an absence of that nagging fear I couldn't seem to shed. For the shepherds and for me, peace has always been a person. The presence of God in the form of a child, sent from the perfection of heaven to an earth wrecked with pain. So the life we'd always dreamed of—heaven—could be accessible to us.

As sweet at those moments were surrounded by my family in a pew, the battle wasn't yet over for me. Fear would still fight for my life, the unpredictable would wreak havoc with my healing. But on December 24, soothed by the music God was crafting from the discordant notes of my life, I felt moored.

I wasn't alone.

CHAPTER 7

New Year, New Fear

My days are swifter than a runner; they fly away.

—JOB 9:25

No one ever told me that grief felt so like fear.

—C. S. LEWIS, *A Grief Observed*

I HAD EVERY INTENTION OF OPENING THE NEW YEAR LIKE A WINdow letting in the sun.

As terrifying as November and December had been, they had culminated in a Christmas of gifts. A negative PET scan. A complication-free surgery. And a pathology report, received the week after surgery, with another reassuring "no evidence of disease."

Nothing but good news. Cancer caught early, and no sign of lymph involvement. My doctor said there was typically a twenty percent chance of recurrence. But without the typical risk factors —smoking, significant alcohol consumption—she thought my odds better. Mine was a best-case scenario. Standard protocol required two-month checkups for two years, followed by three- and six-month checkups until year five. After that, as long as PET scans continued to be clean and we encountered no surprises, she'd pronounce me free and clear.

Like wise men bearing gifts to the Messiah, God delivered a gift: a second chance at life. Thus, I celebrated Christmas with a family I loved more than I imagined possible. We feasted, played, and savored the miracle.

The week after the holidays, having a far brighter outlook on the rest of my life, I packed up both our Christmas decorations and cancer. I was tired of doctor's appointments and mouth pain. With cancer now in the past, I turned and moved into the new year with optimism and enthusiasm.

A big part of that involved diving into my calling and career with renewed passion.

Twenty years before, I'd gone to college with the goal of getting a nursing degree and serving on some kind of mission field. I got the nursing degree and license, but God sent me to a different mission field: as a communicator delivering healing words to hurting people.

In the year or two before cancer, I'd slowly birthed a speaking and writing platform. I'd had several articles, short stories, and devotional meditations published. A few promising speaking engagements dotted my upcoming calendar, including a writers' group in January and my first big-venue event in March—the Hearts at Home Conference in Illinois.

But as I moved deeper into the new year, as two weeks postsurgery turned into four, five, and six, the mouth pain didn't relent as I'd anticipated. I'd assumed my mouth would heal like a scraped knee or cut finger, that each day would bring additional relief and wholeness, and soon I'd see no sign of any wound. After all, the cancer was behind me now. Wasn't it?

The pain didn't go away, in spite of the days that passed. I still had trouble eating, talking, and swallowing. Even an ordinary task like teeth-brushing turned into an endurance sport. Honestly, as

I walked through those first days of January, I started to doubt my future as a public speaker. The low-level chronic pain dogged me. Simple conversations shared within our home posed a challenge. How would I speak for an hour on a stage? How would I shake the hands of new friends, engage in conversations, and offer words of encouragement when words came at such a steep cost?

In spite of my determination to cling to optimism, it was the unrelenting pain that placed me back on the fear rollercoaster. With every chew and swallow, every twinge of discomfort, I wondered if the ulcer—and cancer—had come back.

Then, one unsuspecting day, a look in the mirror revealed two more suspicious spots. Whitish, raw, not far from the initial cancerous lesion.

Uh-oh.

Feeling the fear climb again, I called Dr. Forrester and scheduled her earliest appointment.

She came into my patient room with her characteristic warm smile.

"Good to see you, Michele." She meant it, every time. "So, what's going on?"

I told her about the two spots and the ongoing discomfort. "I wasn't sure what I should do," I apologized, embarrassed to be bothering her, suspecting my presence in her office was nothing but my own paranoia. "I thought you should check it out, just in case."

If she suspected hypochondria or an overactive imagination, she didn't say a word. She simply put on her headlamp, donned a pair of latex gloves, and took a look.

"I don't think it's anything. But we'll biopsy it just to make sure."

I'd been afraid of that. I didn't want to go through another biopsy, more cutting and bleeding. More pain, more healing. More days of isolation and silence.

She ended up taking two samples that day, the process taking only a few minutes.

"I'm pretty sure it's okay, but I'll let you know once I have results. Probably four or five days. Okay?"

No, not okay. But I nodded, tried to mumble my appreciation without giving in to the fear. I wanted to be strong this time. Not the coward I believed I'd been before Christmas.

By the time the elevator let me out at the parking garage, the pain radiated through my throat and down my neck, causing a throbbing pain I couldn't push back. Urgency pushed me toward the safety of my car, and I nearly ran to get there.

Door opened and closed. The world on the outside, the girl on the inside. Then, sitting in the driver's seat of my car in the dark of the parking garage, I lowered my head against the steering wheel and cried.

~

I couldn't have been more than seven years old the day I discovered that Santa Claus isn't real. And, by default, every other magical character I'd ever loved. The Tooth Fairy. The Easter Bunny. Knight Rider.

The truth had been inkling in the back of my childlike and questioning mind. Always practical, I usually could piece together the clues of any surprise to discover it before its revelation. Mysteries were made to be solved, and I loved the unraveling of them.

Until afterward, when, mystery solved, I discovered my insight had cost me my imagination and anticipation.

Such was my experience with Santa Claus. I wanted to know

the truth, and so I asked my parents for it outright. "Are you and Daddy Santa Claus? Are you the ones who do the presents?"

I stood in my parents' bathroom, watching Mom curl and tease her hair. I could tell by her expression that she didn't expect my question. I was too young to be asking it. Always a woman of truth, she delivered it.

"Yes, we are."

And that was the end of my belief in the jolly red dude. But I didn't expect I'd miss him as much as I did.

A cancer diagnosis worked a similar revelation. Before I heard the doctor's words, saw them written on my medical chart, my life passed in holiday, full of presents, feasting, and happy children. I lived ignorant to the drama so many others had already experienced. Divorce had awakened me to the reality of suffering, of the fact that the unexpected can happen, even if you work so very hard to prevent it. Still, cancer remained far off, without the reach to touch my life. I ate healthy, exercised, took care of myself. Besides, I'd achieved my quota of hard things, hadn't I? Lightning doesn't strike the same place twice, right?

Then, like solving the mystery behind Santa's magic, I discovered the morbid reality behind the magic of life.

Lightning is no respecter of persons. Cancer and illness, accidents and death can and will interrupt the holiday. Sometimes more than once. And one day, maybe even today, it will all end. For every one of us.

Of course, I knew this. But now *I knew this*. It scared me. Before November, I didn't question my life or longevity. After November, it was all I could think about. Like the girl who wanted to recapture her belief in Santa, I wanted to go back to my pre-cancer ignorance. The knowing was far too big a weight.

Behind all the fear, grief was the driving emotion. It took me awhile to understand this. I downplayed any loss I felt because I believed I had nothing to grieve. I'd been given good news, hopeful news. But even those with the best-case scenario, those who carry a positive prognosis in their pocket, can't return to the innocence enjoyed before cancer entered the picture. It's too late to unknow the truth.

As I walked through grocery stores and department stores, I watched parents and children, husbands and wives. I noted how they laughed at one another's jokes, how they argued and conversed, played and teased. I watched the bliss of their ignorance, the way cancer didn't touch every single aspect of their ordinary. My tongue moved over the incision, I noted the tightness and twinge of pain, and I envied the magic of their still-mysterious lives.

While "normal" people went through "normal" days, I grew obsessed about cancer-control. While waiting for biopsy results, I ate organic food and drank filtered water. I avoided Diet Coke, trashed the Splenda, and refused the occasional cherished glass of red wine. Anything that might be cancer-causing put me on high alert.

After attending an NBA ball game one night, Troy and I exited the Pepsi Center behind a couple of men who lit up cigarettes the moment we stepped outside. So paralyzed by my fear of more cancer, I held my breath while walking behind them, to a near faint. When I had to take a breath, I covered my nose and mouth with my coat.

Paranoid? A bit. Ridiculous, yet real.

I've talked to countless other cancer survivors, of all extents and varieties. The one commonality we all share is the unexpected grief. Even when we're given a good shot at a long life, even when we have great doctors and the hope of positive outcomes, we experience a deep and profound loss. Cancer is a thief, stealing what we didn't even know we had until it was too late. The innocence is gone, replaced by an acute awareness of the dark flip side of life.

For many, including me, that grief looked a lot like fear.

~

It took a confrontation to finally set me free.

Another day had passed with no phone call or answer. The waiting for biopsy results wore me down. I paced the hardwood floors, dropped to my knees in my closet. The fear routine had become routine, the sick feeling in my stomach far too familiar. I wanted it to end. I wanted to go back to October, before I knew.

Inconsolable, I retreated to my bedroom. I didn't want my boys to see my fear. It embarrassed me, shamed me. I wanted them to think me strong.

Still, afraid of being alone, I leaned my head out the door and called my husband to me. Again.

"Troy, can you come here a minute?"

I heard him walking, steady, taking one stair at a time. When he opened the bedroom door, his face showed no trace of the anxiety I felt. He didn't share my despair, nor did he fear for my life.

It ticked me off.

"How are you so calm? Why aren't you worried?"

We'd had this conversation before, and I'd peppered him with the same frustrated questions. I knew it wearied him, but he never let on.

"Because you're going to be fine. I'm sorry you have to go through this, but you're going to be okay."

Fear blinds. I couldn't see any reason for his peace. So I

resisted his attempt at reassurance with another sharp and pointed question.

"But what if? What if I'm not okay? What if the worst-case scenario happens?"

Last time I'd checked, Troy wasn't God. He couldn't make promises about life and death. He couldn't control the outcomes. I slung a little snark and waited to see what he'd do with it.

Then, sitting together on our bed, he spoke the words that finally broke fear's chokehold on me: "If you really believe what you say you believe, Michele, then it's only going to get better for you from here."

Whoa. I didn't expect that.

I didn't expect to be reminded of the faith I'd claimed since childhood. To be challenged to either believe it and live it, or let it go.

If I really believe ...

Did I believe what I claimed? For years I'd professed a solid and sure faith, to my husband and children, neighbors and friends, and in venues and on platforms in front of hundreds of strangers. I talked about God as if he were real and powerful and interested in his children. And I talked about heaven as my ultimate vacation destination. But somehow I'd let cancer turn God into Santa Claus, a childish fantasy and a work of fiction. I still believed *in* him. I just didn't *believe him*. I didn't count on him to be the powerful, rescuing, interested God in the middle of my crisis. Mine was a belief that looked good on paper, but didn't work itself out in reality.

And flimsy belief gives birth to fear, not courage.

Troy's question was a valid one, a difficult one, and one I needed to answer. I could either hang on to fear or hold on to my faith. But I could not hang on to both. As I sat on the bed next to my husband, I felt his question—and its implications—work its way into me like the key to a rusty lock. I wrestled with it, worked it around in my head until I felt the pop of the lock and myself set free.

Yes. Yes, I believe.

Just the thought, those three words held in heart and mind, warmed me slowly and surely like the first swallow of Earl Grey on a cold day. Hope gets the final word in my life. From the moment I chose Jesus, life trumped death. But somewhere in my thirty-nine years, my love affair with this life had eclipsed my anticipation of the next. Living had become my idol, more the object of my worship than the Lifegiver himself.

It's a difficult tension, living with one hand embracing earth and the other reaching for the eternal. To think only of heaven is to miss out on the gift of life. And to dwell on this life is to miss out on the grandeur—and anticipation—of what is yet to come. Instead, I needed to see heaven and earth through the lens of the other. Only then could I embrace the glorious hues of both.

I huddled in my bedroom, still fragile but far less afraid. I'd been given the gift of a single life, one I was to embrace, celebrate, and receive with joy. But the end of the gift was never meant to be the end of the story. Only the beginning of one.

"Therefore we do not lose heart. Though outwardly we are wasting away, yet inwardly we are being renewed day by day. For our light and momentary troubles are achieving for us an eternal glory that far outweighs them all. So we fix our eyes not on what is seen, but on what is unseen, since what is seen is temporary, but what is unseen is eternal."[12]

CHAPTER 8

The Strength of Empty

Heroes didn't leap tall buildings or stop bullets with an outstretched hand; they didn't wear boots and capes. They bled, and they bruised, and their superpowers were as simple as listening, or loving. Heroes were ordinary people who knew that even if their own lives were impossibly knotted, they could untangle someone else's. And maybe that one act could lead someone to rescue you right back.

—JODI PICOULT, *Second Glance*

CANCER WORKS LIKE A BUG LIGHT. ANNOUNCE A DIAGNOSIS, AND similar stories and scenarios swarm your direction.

"My brother was just diagnosed with stage 4 liver cancer. They don't think he's going to make it."

"My mom was cancer-free for years. Then it came back. It was awful."

And my personal favorite: "My friend was diagnosed with the same kind of cancer as you. He died a few months ago."

Thank you. Super helpful.

Emails, Facebook messages, phone calls, and texts. Day after day, the stories swarmed. My heart wanted to pray for each need, wanted to reach out to each person who suffered. Many had prayed for me, had pushed past their discomfort to reach out. Prayer and presence had carried me through.

But the swarming overwhelmed me. Not the encouraging, hopeful, uplifting stories so much as the doom and gloom ones. I never made a big cancer announcement, didn't post anything publicly, online, until more than a year later. But those close to me knew, and word spread. I'd joined the cancer club, willing or not. Once people heard, they shared their club-member stories. Cancer creates unusual alliances.

Paul said, "Praise be to the God and Father of our Lord Jesus Christ, the Father of compassion and the God of all comfort, who comforts us in all our troubles, so that we can comfort those in any trouble with the comfort we ourselves receive from God."[13] I believed this to be true, even anticipated the day when my regrettable experience became a nice, neat story I could pull out like a Hallmark card offering to those in a hard place.

But I couldn't do it. Not yet. I still felt raw, fragile, so very weak. I didn't know it then, but I was still in a post-trauma state, my emotions and thoughts on high alert. On the flip side of the initial adrenaline and intensity sat a steep decline into grief and loss. I vacillated between the two, and all it took was the mention of the word cancer for me to be launched back into high alert.

In addition to the cancer stories, I received countless offers of advice and certain cures.

"Don't eat sugar. Cancer loves sugar."

"It's the pesticides. That's why cancer is epidemic right now. Organic. It's the only way to go."

"Take this vitamin. It's a cure, even if the FDA doesn't approve it. And be sure to start juicing."

And don't forget to eat a pound of broccoli at every meal,

turn around in a circle twenty-eight times, and chew gum while standing on your head and rubbing your stomach.

Whoa, baby. I appreciated all the well-intentioned counsel. For a while, I ate broccoli, avoided sugar, took vitamins, and nearly took out a second mortgage to buy organic food. All healthy choices. Regardless of the anticancer potential, I knew it was good for my body.

But it also fed the fear monster. I worried about drinking tap water, certain the treatment chemicals were dangerous. I fretted while taking long walks outside, afraid Denver's air pollution upped my chances of a recurrence. I wondered whether my hair spray and hair coloring were loading my body with toxic chemicals. Each day became an impossible maze of decisions that could take me either toward or away from cancer. Crazy-making.

For fifteen years, my parents lived in the suburbs of Chicago. Every time we went for a visit, we trekked into the city to visit Navy Pier and maybe catch a Cubs game. But before we'd load up in the car, Mom or Dad checked traffic, to see about "gaper delays."

"Gaper delays?" I asked the first time. "What in the world is that?" Sounded like a rash.

"You know, gapers. People who can't take their eyes off a car accident. They hit their brakes, trying to get a look at the carnage. It backs up traffic."

The thought horrified me. And yet, when we drove into the city, we almost always encountered a gaper delay of some kind.

My life as a so-called cancer survivor created a gaper delay. I couldn't move forward because of all the conversations and stories that slowed and stopped, pulled me back to fear. Well-meaning friends wanted to know my prognosis, pain levels, and outlook. They expressed concern for my significant weight loss, commenting on my sunken face, the dark circles under my eyes, and my baggy jeans. Others gave abundant advice. Still others wanted to dump their personal heartache on someone who understood.

I loved that they cared, appreciated all the good intention. But all this cancer talk created a couple of problems. First, talking itself was a problem. To answer the endless phone calls and questions caused pain and cost valuable healing time. Second, I was sick and tired of being sick. I didn't want to talk about cancer anymore. Instead, I wanted to pretend it didn't happen, package it up like a donation to Goodwill and drop it off for someone else. Cancer sat like a black hole in my history. I wanted to move forward, reclaim the life I'd enjoyed before I got sucked into the nightmare.

Everywhere I turned, however, cancer showed up. Do you know how many commercials advertise cancer treatments? How many movies have a character with cancer? Facebook is a gold mine of cancer survivors and stories. A great place for support and connection, but a field of land mines for a girl who wants to live.

Gaper delays. I couldn't move forward.

That's why, as I prepped to return to the speaking circuit, I decided to keep my cancer story to myself. I would avoid talking about my health at all costs. I couldn't handle the swarming.

I'd had a couple of small speaking engagements in January and February. I smiled, nodded, did my job without any indication that something horrific had happened. It worked, for the most part. I could pretend for those brief public appearances.

But March brought my first large speaking engagement. The Hearts at Home Conference. Six thousand moms gathered on the Illinois State University campus in central Illinois. I'd been asked to deliver two sessions two times each to hundreds of women.

The invitation came months before my diagnosis. I'd been

thrilled at the opportunity. This was my first big break. I imagined it could help propel my speaking platform unlike any other speaking engagement before.

But then everything changed two days before Thanksgiving. I no longer cared about platforms, big breaks, and making a name for myself. I just wanted to live. To be with those I loved. And I definitely didn't want to talk about cancer. It'd already stolen enough of the spotlight.

I almost canceled the engagement. I'd become a woman afraid to leave her home. I limped through each day, needing Troy's reassurances moment by moment. The thought of flying to another state and being in a room with thousands of strangers overwhelmed me. I wasn't sure I could do it.

Then the unexpected happened. Again. Not a major crisis, but the camel's straw that made his load too big to bear.

Exactly one week before the conference kicked off, I noticed a tooth starting to ache. I'd never had a toothache before and didn't know what to think. Maybe I'd bitten down on something wrong. Then again, I'd had months of mouth pain. Maybe this was another side effect of all the trauma?

By Saturday morning, two days later, the pain turned unbearable. A visit to a high-priced, weekend dentist confirmed the problem: an abscessed tooth. I'd need to see a specialist about a root canal. But they wouldn't open again until Monday. To get through the weekend, he prescribed an antibiotic.

"You should feel better in twenty-four hours," he said.

He was wrong.

What followed was a long and extremely painful forty-eight hours. By Monday morning, I awoke to an abscess that would make the strongest stomach turn. I paced, in agony, cell phone in hand, waiting for the strike of eight to call the endodontic specialist's office.

By early afternoon, I was a new woman. My first root canal. And contrary to the stream of horror stories I'd heard before, it brought nothing but relief. After four solid days of excruciating pain, I could finally rest.

Only one problem. All the mouth drama had rubbed raw the surgical area that hadn't fully healed. Plus, I now sported yet another open wound where the abscess had been. In forty-eight hours, I'd board a plane to central Illinois and six thousand women who loved to chat. Four speaking sessions. Hours meeting attendees at a book table. And once again, I was eating pureed food and unable to talk.

I'm convinced God has a sense of humor. No doubt about it. I told him he needed new material.

~

By the time I landed in Bloomington, Illinois, and checked into my hotel that Thursday, I had nothing to give.

Chronic pain is a drain. I'd hit a local Walgreens to buy hydrogen peroxide for mouth rinses. (If you've never done a peroxide rinse, *don't*.) I gargled warm salt water and popped three Advil every four to six hours, without fail. I hoped I could talk by the time I reached the venue.

In addition to my physical limitations, I had little emotional reserves. The previous months' rollercoaster of emotions and experiences had zapped my strength. And my family, my rock of Gibraltar, was a thousand miles away. Intellectually, I recognized this speaking opportunity as a privilege. Someone believed in me and my message, or I wouldn't be there.

Snap out of it, Michele!

How does one snap out of a deep, swallowing hole? Alone in my hotel room, I could think only of how much I wanted to go home. I missed the safety of the familiar. I feared the unknown that awaited me the next day and doubted I had it in me to fulfill my job. Even as I wrestled with pain and homesickness, I chastised my selfishness.

The next day, thousands of women would gather, hungry and hopeful, waiting for some kind of offering from empty me.

God, I have nothing. Nothing. You're going to have to show up in a big way. The Advil too. I don't know how I'm going to do this.

Every now and then, a particular Bible passage haunts me. In the months preceding the cancer diagnosis, Romans 12:1–2 had been one of those passages. It showed up when I listened to the radio. Made an appearance in the devotional I read. Flashed on the screen during the pastor's Sunday sermon. Appeared tucked in an email delivered to my inbox. For months, Romans 12:1–2 became like a neighbor who wouldn't go away—knocking, knocking, knocking on my front door until I finally opened it up.

"Therefore, I urge you, brothers and sisters, in view of God's mercy, to offer your bodies as a living sacrifice, holy and pleasing to God—this is your true and proper worship. Do not conform to the pattern of this world, but be transformed by the renewing of your mind. Then you will be able to test and approve what God's will is—his good, pleasing and perfect will."

Isn't that nice.

I had no idea what it meant. Or what God wanted me to do with it. But it wouldn't leave me alone.

Romans 12. Romans 12. Romans 12.

When cancer showed up, I assumed the reference had something to do with my new circumstance, as if God wanted to use it to prepare me for this new thing. "Renewing my mind" made a modicum of sense. I needed to get control of my fear, change how I allowed myself to think and process my circumstances.

Okay, got it. Check.

Other than that, I hadn't a clue. Offering my body as a living sacrifice? A spiritual act of worship?

Pretend this is Pictionary, God. I need more clues.

I didn't expect the means of his revealing.

Somehow, I pulled myself together in my hotel room and started the long walk to the conference center. I needed to set up my book table and meet the event hosts.

Erika greeted me. A spunky, dark-haired woman with a smile two miles wide. She extended her hand and introduced herself.

"Hi, Michele. I'm Erika. Nice to meet you!"

Fun and sassy. I could peg it with those first exchanged words. I liked her right away.

With Erika leading the way, I hauled my computer bag and purse across the product floor and to my book table. It sat in the center of a gigantic ballroom, a room that would be filled with booths, speakers, and thousands of chatty moms soon enough. In between speaking sessions, I'd sit at my table, along with a dozen other speakers. My home base for the weekend.

It took me most of an hour to arrange the table with books, business cards, and freebies. Then, pain. The Advil was wearing off, again. Pulling three more out of my purse, I abandoned the book table in search of a water fountain.

That's when I heard Erika's voice behind me.

"Michele, hold on," she hissed, a whisper with the volume of urgency. Then she grabbed my behind. Yes, *Erika's* hand on *my* derriere.

"Excuse me?" I jumped, might've slapped her hand. We didn't know each other that well.

"Hold on a minute." She maintained her grip on my backside. "You lost your skirt."

What?!

"Your skirt fell. I'm pulling it back up."

Sure enough. The long, chocolate brown skirt I'd meticulously ironed and donned an hour or two before had fallen well below the tree line. In a wide open ballroom filled with no less than thirty conference staff and speakers preparing for their event, I'd revealed the lesser half of my body.

Isn't that nice.

How embarrassing. I wanted to impress these people, appear every bit the polished and professional speaker they'd hired me to be. Ahem. I might've missed that mark.

Offer your body as a living sacrifice.

Romans 12:1–2. Again. You've got to be kidding me.

Okay. Fine. I get it. But cut me a little slack here. My skirt?

I imagine he laughed, deep and rumbly. Full of mirth and absent mockery. I believe he laughs more than we think.

A living sacrifice. Holy and pleasing, Michele.

But I'm a mess. Empty, in pain. Nothing to give. I feel more afraid than faithful.

Exactly. I'm with you.

What had started with my mortification ended up becoming my salvation. Dignity was officially off the table. Polish and perfection didn't bother to show up. But grace was very much on the table. All I could offer was me, as empty and lost as I was. And it turned out to be exactly what those beautiful, precious moms needed. Me too.

In the end, my weekend with the women of Hearts at Home

became my first big step toward my postcancer ministry life, giving me a hint of the redemption that can come when you dare to dive into the dark places with those who suffer there. For two days, women who heard my story lined up at my book table, one by one sharing their own stories of heartache: of broken marriages, wayward children, and the difficult wrestlings of this life of faith. Again and again, I abandoned a chair to grasp hands with a stranger, close my eyes, and pray. Together we poured out our hearts to a God we desperately needed but didn't always understand. Real, broken, in-progress women trying so very hard to live. In those moments, far from the safety of my home and family, the veil between heaven and earth thinned. A rare gift, and one I would've missed had I canceled my flight and stayed at home.

Erika and I laughed about the skirt malfunction all weekend, as did the traumatized eyewitnesses, no doubt. My presentations weren't flawless. Exhaustion and pain still hovered. But I discovered something as I talked and prayed with the equally broken, weary, and in-pain women whose paths crossed mine: authenticity ministers far more than put-togetherness. And vulnerability builds a far stronger bond than perfection.

There is strength in empty. Not the kind of strength we wish for. We want polished strength, the kind that wears a cape and leaps tall buildings with a single bound. I couldn't leap or fly or save anyone from catastrophe. In fact, I could barely show up. But I did. Show up. And that ended up being a strength all of its own.

Ministry—of the truest kind—isn't about impressing unknown strangers with spotless presentations and a flawless life. It's about exposing the hidden imperfections and giving others permission to do the same. Becoming a fellow struggler who delivers zero judgment but abundant grace.

Few things display unadulterated beauty like a pouring out when you've nothing to give. It must come from an otherworldly place, a well whose source you do not control. In that weak and lonely place of utter dependency, I learned a little bit about what it means to be a living sacrifice. It is a pure, holy, and sacred offering. Simply because you have nothing to do with it.

A spiritual act of worship.

Even when—especially when—your skirt falls to the floor.

CHAPTER 9

Hammer Blows and Houses That Stand

Character is not born of stillness.
It requires the hammer blows of affliction.
—CHARLES R. SWINDOLL

My dad said I must've been five or six years old at the time. Stubborn as a rusted bolt, even then. His words, not mine.

Hammer in one hand, my little-girl fingers gripped a thick silver nail in the other. Dad, a natural carpenter, stood to the side, working on a table or bookshelf or some other wood project of his own. He could build just about anything with a block of wood. To this day, I love the smell of wood shavings and the burnt smell of a working saw. It still makes me think of him.

I knelt in the grass in front of one of his scraps, face set. I wanted to be strong like Daddy, a maker of something beautiful.

Brow furrowed, I placed the nail square on the board. My right hand gripped the heavy old hammer and pulled back for a mighty six-year-old swing.

Whoosh!

I missed the nail by an inch. Maybe more, considering the dent in the board. Determined, I gave it another go. This time I came close enough to whack my finger. Tears threatened, but I swallowed them down. I couldn't cry, not with Daddy close by.

Instead, I pulled myself back up, grabbed the hammer, and tried again.

And again.

And again.

I lost track of how many swings and misses. Each time my determination grew more fierce. Until the last time. I really thought I was going to do it that time. Which is why, when the hammer missed and the nail toppled, I exploded in frustration.

"I can't do it!" I wailed, throwing both the nail and the hammer onto the ground. "It's too hard!"

Daddy didn't stop, even though I knew he heard my rant. He kept working, not saying a word. For half a minute, he simply let me pout. Then he put his own hammer down, turned, and looked at me with an intensity I'll never forget.

"Stop saying 'can't.'" He crossed his arms, unyielding. "You're not a quitter, Michele. Get back up and try again. Now."

I was so mad at him for that. I needed comfort, not confrontation. Truth is I wanted him to feel sorry for me, to understand my pain and give me reason to walk away. Instead, he called me on my lack of courage. Demanded that I keep swinging.

There was no arguing with Daddy. Not then, not now. Seething, defeated, I picked up the hammer one more time. It wouldn't matter. One more swing wouldn't bring me success.

Whoosh!

Wouldn't you know it. That was the swing that drove the nail into the board.

I could probably count on one hand the number of times I've quit anything. I'm stubborn and strong-willed to a fault, like a bulldog with his teeth sunk into a prize. But in the spring after cancer, I had little chops left for much of anything.

Within a week of returning from the Hearts at Home Conference, I knew something was wrong. Underneath my tongue, where January's biopsies had been cut out, a small quarter-inch purplish bubble had formed. It looked like a balloon filled with water, growing in the soft, tender tissue hidden in the floor of my mouth. About the size of my pinkie fingernail. Each day, it grew bigger, looking more and more taut, as if it might burst. Only it didn't. Instead, pain radiated down my throat and neck.

No. Please, no.

It didn't take my nursing degree to know this wasn't supposed to happen. Weary of calling my doctor with complaints (and half afraid of her answer), I shot off an email message. Less intrusive, I thought. She replied quickly, asking me to take a picture and send it.

Now trust me when I say shooting a picture of the inside of your mouth is neither easy nor attractive. I had to open wide like a yawning hippopotamus, finagle my smart phone inside, and—hold it—*snap!* Definitely social media material. Or not.

After evaluating the pic, she told me to watch it for another week or two, let her know if the bubble changed size.

It didn't take more than a few days to see it had grown considerably. Without any other recourse, I called her office and set another appointment, dreading it in my bones. I didn't want yet another knife-wielding procedure, didn't want more pain followed by baby-food dinners.

But that's exactly what happened.

In April.

And July.

And again in August.

I had three more surgeries that year. Each time, the balloon-like cyst grew bigger than before. Each time, I resisted and ranted against it. Then, spent, I called the doctor, endured another out-patient procedure, and returned home to soft food, pain pills, and weeks of slow healing.

Those long, unending months drained me in every way. My clothes hung off my body like a child in her mama's dress. At my lowest, I weighed 124 pounds, far less than usual for my five-foot-seven-inch athletic frame. My face hollowed, dark circles rounding my eyes, as much from exhaustion as from the chronic fear that wouldn't let me go.

I hated it, both the fear of another blow and the aloneness it created. Some days it hit me head-on, like a hurricane wind, laying me flat and keeping me from moving forward. On the good days, it hovered like background noise I couldn't quite ignore, leaving me agitated and on edge. Unpredictability dictated my day-to-day life. Each twinge of pain came with a question mark: had the cancer come back? Like the girl swinging her hammer and always missing the nail, I didn't want to do it anymore.

Why, God? I keep praying and pleading. I keep asking you for relief. Why won't you do something?

I never received an answer from him. No divine memo explaining why he didn't swoop in and save the day. With a word or a single thought, he could've commanded the pain to stop, my body to heal. He holds the oceans in his hands, sets the earth to spinning, and weaves cells together into human form. Why wouldn't he conquer this cyst for me? Was it too much to ask?

To this day, I don't understand why God didn't wave his magic wand and give me relief. However, in the absence of a holy revelation, I finally came closer to a medical one.

The cyst had likely formed as a result of January's biopsies. I'd gone to Dr. Forrester's office that day consumed with fear and worry over a couple of suspicious spots. I suspect she performed the biopsies as much to assuage my fear as for any medical necessity.

In the process, those incisions interrupted the path of the salivary glands under my tongue. As a result, they weren't draining as they should, instead forming a pool. A large cyst in the floor of my mouth. All because of two biopsies.

The only fix? Perform a marsupialization, a fileting open of the cyst tissue to allow the area to heal correctly from the inside out.

"The body knows what to do," Dr. Forrester had said. "We just have to give it a chance to heal itself. As many times as necessary."

As many times as necessary proved to be many more than once.

For the first time, I understood the emotion behind Paul's words in 2 Corinthians 12: "Three times I pleaded with the Lord to take it away from me," he said. Like me, Paul asked the God he trusted for relief. Again and again. From what? We don't know, and it doesn't really matter. But it was difficult enough for him to label it "a thorn in my flesh, a messenger of Satan, to torment me."[14]

Tormented. Yes, that's it exactly. I felt tormented by the unrelenting pain and fear. I wanted to close the cancer chapter, leave it behind and run full force back into life and health. But each time healing neared, something cut me wide open again. Every time I found new strength to keep moving forward, another unexpected circumstance crushed me.

Whoosh!

What's wrong with me?

Whoosh!

Why won't you fix this?

Whoosh!

It's too hard. I'm done.

Unlike the horrific pain and grief of so many in this broken world, my crisis wasn't life threatening or terminal. All along, I understood this. It wasn't a fatal car accident, the death of a child, or a famine in India.

Still, given enough time, even a termite can take a house down.

Months of pain and uncertainty wore away my faith. Like a constant dripping, circumstances eroded my resolve. Just as my clothes hung off my frame, I shrank to a fraction of my former self. No longer strong. No longer determined. Instead, I wallowed in the enormity of my circumstance and my inability to control the outcome. I didn't have the strength or will to pull back the hammer and keep swinging.

April 6, a few short weeks after an abscess, a root canal, and a Hearts at Home Conference, I once again found myself on a cold operating table in Dr. Forrester's procedure room. She called in two nurses to assist. I was to be numbed, but not sedated. It will take only a half hour, she said. Just relax, rest. Then you'll be on your way home.

Rest? If only.

I curled up on my right side, right arm underneath my head, mouth open, so Dr. Forrester could do her work. I couldn't talk. Couldn't cry. Instead tears, silent and plentiful, fell in rivers down my cheeks and my tucked arm to drench the table that was holding me up.

"Are you okay?" One of the nurses looked at me, confused by the tears. The surgeon hadn't done anything yet. "Is she okay?" He turned to Dr. Forrester when I didn't respond.

Didn't he know I couldn't talk?

God, please. No more.

In the book of Matthew, Jesus tells a story about two carpenters. One foolish and the other wise. The first, dreaming of an ocean view, built his house on a beach. Sand and water as far as the eye could see.

The other builder, more practical than pampered, opted for a higher foundation, building his house on stone rather than sand. The rocks didn't come with an ocean view. A true carpenter, he knew what mattered was not so much the view out the window as what lay underneath the floor.

Both houses went up without a hitch, both men swinging hammers like experts. Soon, each man moved in and made a home. All was well, both on the sand and on the stone.

Until unexpected weather hit.

In a flash, the beach house fell. The builder's best efforts washed away.

As for the house built on stone? It endured the same weather, the same relentless beating. Even so, it did not fall. All because of the solid rock underneath.

From the moment of my diagnosis, through the scans, blood tests, and surgeries, I sought to find my rest by building a place with a view. I wanted to see into the future, to predict the outcome of my life and gain a sense of peace based on what I could see. Simply, I wielded worry as a means to control.

A house on sand.

But rather than control my circumstances, my circumstances controlled me. I focused on the view and, in the process, forgot about my foundation.

Thirty-three verses before Jesus' story of the wise and foolish builders, he said words that held the key to saving me: "Who of you by worrying can add a single hour to your life?"[15]

Boy, I sure tried. Fooled by both panic and pain, I convinced myself that worry gave me a measure of control. From morning until night, I attempted to worry myself into wholeness, as if preparing for the worst would guard me from any unwanted surprises. I'd had enough of those.

Only it didn't. Worry, like cancer, consumes life, eating away at a person from the inside out. It exaggerates the unknown and clouds the known until the worried person sees only the horror of what might be, rather than the beauty of what already is.

In his mercy, even as I lay on the cold surgical table, God pulled me back to the only foundation that could weather my storm.

"My grace is sufficient for you, for my power is made perfect in weakness."[16]

Not a house with a view of the future but a house with a foundation that won't fail. God's presence in the here and now. A promise never to leave, never to give way. Stone, not sand.

"That is why, for Christ's sake, I delight in weaknesses, in insults, in hardships, in persecutions, in difficulties. For when I am weak, then I am strong."[17]

I opened my mouth, waiting for the doctor to cut me open once again. Tears still fell, and I felt anything but strong. Instead, exhausted and ready to quit. Even so, God stood near. I like to imagine he caught the tears that fell, holding them in those strong, calloused carpenter's hands of his.

Then he looked at me with an intensity that trumped my own.

Quitting is easy, Michele. But I dare you to live. Whether you have fifty days or fifty years, don't waste them worrying. Stop saying "can't." Pick up that hammer and live!

CHAPTER 10

Un-Mother's Day

Love sought is good, but giv'n unsought is better.
—SHAKESPEARE, *Twelfth Night*

SEVENTEEN HOURS. GIVE OR TAKE.

That's how long our honeymoon lasted. Leaving our three small boys in the care of their grandparents, Troy and I left our picture-perfect wedding venue late on a Sunday night and drove to Winter Park, Colorado. Tucked in the woods near the ski resort, a studio condo waited for us.

Our first night as husband and wife.

Seventeen hours later, we drove back down the mountain to Denver to pick up three boys after school.

To start math homework and spelling words.

That, my friends, is how our marriage began.

Insanity. I-N-S-A-N-I-T-Y.

There was no gradual getting used to marriage. No slow warm-up to the idea of children and family. Instead, "I do" followed by a headfirst dive into the deep end of the parenting pool.

That is why counselors, pastors, and pretty much everyone who breathes recommends you marry *before* having children. Not after.

I've heard couples describe something they term "the honeymoon phase" of their marriage. When they do, eyes sparkle and cheeks flush. They lean in close and look at each other with secret-keeping in their eyes. It's disgusting.

Okay, fine. It's sweet. But here's the deal: Troy and I never had a honeymoon phase. After our wedding day, my eyes moistened and cheeks flushed too. But for entirely different reasons. And not in a happy, I'm-so-in-love way.

It took a giant blue teacup for me to recognize our new family for what it was. What it *is*.

The trip had been a surprise, something Troy and I plotted behind closed doors. We spent a year's worth of savings knowing we'd stand for hours in long lines for rides that would last seconds. But this is what crazy parents do for the children they claim to love: they take them to Disneyland.

The night before we left, we packed the car with bulging bags and suitcases, while the boys slept without a clue of the adventure awaiting them at dawn. In the morning, we all climbed into Troy's Izuzu Trooper (remember those?) under the pretense of running errands. The boys chattered in the back while Troy and I stole secret glances. It wasn't until we arrived at the airport that we revealed hidden suitcases and plane tickets.

How would you like to go to Disneyland?!

Woohoo! Yeehaw! Hip-hip-hooray!

For a solid week, we followed our three hyperactive, grade-school boys across the full expanse of California's theme park. They'd never been before and wanted to see it all. Along with every other family in the United States, it seemed. Even in September, people filled every inch of the park, mothers and fathers, grandmothers and grandfathers with adorable children sporting Mickey Mouse ears and princess tutus.

As I remember it, in the late afternoon, I took my oldest stepson, Tyler, to the Mad Tea Party ride while Troy took the younger two, Ryan and Jacob, on something less likely to cause vomiting. While we waited in another long line, making microscopic centipede steps forward, I attempted to make conversation.

What's been your favorite ride so far?

Dunno.

Are you having fun?

I guess.

What should we ride next?

I don't care.

Exhilarating.

Slowly, ever so slowly, we approached the front of the line. Only a couple of shiny, smiling mothers and their children preceded us, followed by a long stretch of others winding through silver cattle fencing behind. It made for a storybook's illustrations, all these faces plastered with glee. After all, Disneyland is the happiest place on earth.

Finally, our turn came. I looked to the sprightly Disney employee waiting to direct us onto the platform of swirling teacups. Rather than address me, she bent down to look my boy eye-to-eye: "You and your mom can get in the blue teacup, right over there."

She smiled and pointed as she said it, delivering her announcement with perk, like a wrapped present topped with a bright red bow. I couldn't help smiling in return. *You and your mom*. I loved the sound of those words.

I reached for my boy and started to move through the turnstile. And that's when his shriek interrupted my bliss.

"SHE'S NOT MY MOM!"

Wha . . . ?

There, in the happiest place on earth and inches from giant-sized, magical teacups, I shrank to the barest fraction of myself. If I could've found a hole to crawl into, I would have. Instead, I stood transfixed and mortified. Embarrassed. In front of hundreds of perfect traditional mothers and fathers, my stepson exposed me as an imposter.

His stepmom.

In a second, we went from happy family to fake family.

That's when I knew: no matter how many blue teacups we share, no matter how much I love his father and wish it to be different, I am not—and never will be—his mother.

~

Although I'm sure those early months of our new marriage and stepfamily had glimmers of bliss, what I mostly recall is how very hard it was. And how it wasn't at all what I'd imagined. If I thought single motherhood had been characterized by exhaustion and thankless effort, a second marriage with three children took both to a new level of discomfort.

About the time I thought I'd figured it out and had learned from my plentiful mistakes, our sweet angel boys turned into teenagers. Overnight, the rules changed, and I didn't have a clue. Any progress we'd made seemed to disappear. Instead, mood swings. Conflict. Disconnect. Some days, I thought it would kill me. Other days, I hoped it would.

You should know I enjoy teenagers, love hanging out with them. For years, I was a youth sponsor in the high school youth group. I led a small group and mentored students almost every week. During the summer, I went on youth trips, up to two weeks at a time on a chartered bus with more than sixty hot and hormonal students. On purpose. I felt value in that space.

Except when it came to my own teenagers.

Then I felt inept.

The tension escalated soon after Tyler turned sixteen. On the outside, he seemed a typical teenager, happy even. He had his driver's license, was doing well in school, and was involved in the church youth group.

But at home, where emotion wasn't so easily masked, he seemed irritated and angry more often than not. Later I came to recognize this as fairly typical for adolescence. At the time, I just knew he hated our rules, resisted being told what to do, didn't want to show respect or consideration for his brothers or his dad and me.

So we called him on it. He didn't like it.

And so, one unsuspecting Monday, he didn't come home. I'd been working all day in my home office, writing, cooking, and doing whatever else occupied those routine days. I remember glancing at the clock midway through the afternoon.

Tyler should be home from school by now.

But he wasn't. Dread quickened my pulse, my heart knowing the truth before my head did. I checked my phone, scanned for a text message.

Nothing.

The bus had come and gone. Other kids had already disappeared behind their front doors, scavenging for snacks, maybe telling someone about their day.

My kitchen remained absent one boy.

I texted him. No response.

I texted Troy. He hadn't heard from him either.

Maybe an hour or two later, our son finally answered his

phone. Simply put, he wasn't coming home. Sick of our boundaries, he was going to live with another relative, a place with more freedom, he said.

And just like that, we went from being a family of five to a family of four.

Every day following—every single day—I tortured myself with impossible questions: *How did this happen? Where did we go wrong? If we'd been the right kind of parents—if I'd been the right kind of stepmother—he wouldn't have left, right? This is my fault. How do I fix it?*

No matter how hard I prayed, I couldn't unravel the tangle of knots. Though Troy grieved, our son's absence was particularly difficult on me. His choice to leave felt personal, a pointed rejection of me as a person and mother. I'd failed him.

Years later, after parenting two more teenagers with their own struggles, I realized that much of his rebellion and our conflict were simply a normal part of a child's transition from childhood to adulthood. A part of parenting adolescents and learning to let them go.

But it took me a long time to stop seeing it all as my fault.

~

The Mother's Day after cancer, I woke up in Syracuse, New York. Two thousand miles from my husband and children.

I'd been invited to be the guest speaker for DeWitt Community Church's three weekend services. The invitation felt awkward to me. Didn't my stepfamily status exclude me from expertise on the topics of motherhood and family? Hadn't I blown my chance when I ended up divorced? Why would a church ask a woman with my background to speak on Mother's Day?

That was precisely the reason Dr. Mark Sommers invited me to come.

"Broken families are more the norm than the exception anymore," he told me through the phone. I cringed at the "broken family" reference, the label I couldn't shed. Still, I knew he spoke the truth.

"Your story is real and authentic," he continued. "You can deliver the message with a credibility and perspective many others can't."

Wow. I accepted the invitation. My background didn't disqualify me from ministry but created a unique opportunity for it. His affirmation gave me validation and boldness I hadn't yet experienced. Perhaps others, like Mark, believed redemption could reach even the divorced. To that point, I hadn't discovered many.

My message was simple: the power of a mother's influence as evidenced in the portraits of three of history's notable mothers: Monica, mother of St. Augustine; Susanna Wesley, mother of John and Charles; and Corrie ten Boom, who never married or had children of her own but who "mothered" many of us through her example of faith and forgiveness during the Holocaust. I chose expected and unexpected women, for good reason.

I also offered a fourth portrait: my own. An unglamorous mothering journey through childbirth, divorce, single-mothering, remarriage, and step-mothering. It was a moment of uncomfortable and oh-so-public honesty. Like finding your skirt tucked inside your underwear. Humorous, maybe, but mostly humiliating.

As I held up framed black-and-white portraits of Monica, Susanna, and Corrie and told their stories, I thought of our family portrait back at home. It hung above the family room fireplace, wrapped in a three-inch, chunky black frame with silver brocade etching swirling around the edge. The smiling faces of father, mother, and three boys.

The photograph captured a younger us, taken two or three years past. Thick trees of Denver's Observatory Park surrounded us as we sat on lush grass wearing jeans and coordinating shirts. Tyler sat on the left, seventeen years old, a senior in high school. Ryan, a junior at the time, sat on the right with one knee in the grass and the other propped under his elbow. Jacob, twelve, smiled front and center, his face filled with still-sweet-as-ice-cream innocence. And Troy and I sat in the middle, sandwiched by our children, my hand on his knee and his arm an anchor around my back. We smiled, of course. The photographer told us to.

Framed familial happiness on a fireplace mantel.

This is how we displayed our family to the world. Posed and edited perfection. But I knew the truth. I saw the details that didn't make it into the frame. The years of grieving our former families while trying to cleave to a new marriage and stepfamily. The long hard work of learning how to let go of what was lost and grab onto what was gained. And then the years during which our admiring little boys turned disgruntled teenagers, and how that change left us frustrated, exhausted, and screaming at each other more than loving each other. And how, after the dust had settled, we emerged less a portrait-ready family and more five separate individuals licking wounds and trying to figure out where we go from here.

I shared all of this from my place on the stage, a purging and exposing that both unnerved and relieved me. And then I shared the tenderest part, the piece I'd held back and guarded for months.

Mothering when you hear a doctor say the word cancer.

With that single word, the entire room stilled. Men, women, and children collectively held their breath. I'd soon learn this is the typical response to any kind of cancer pronouncement. It isn't a word we like to hear, so we shrink back. It reminds us we are, in fact, mortal, and this life—and the people we love—will not last forever.

Cancer, as terrifying as it was, forced me to wrestle with my mothering, I said. Had I done enough? Had I been the kind of mother I wanted to be? This was both an excruciating and inspiring exercise, to look at the role I cherished most through the magnifying glass of limited time to see what impact, if any, I'd had.

I used to believe, back when my children were small and I managed their contained little worlds, that the worth of a mother is measured by the behavior of her children. A good mom raises good children who make good choices. Any other result reflects poorly on the mother herself.

Then my children grew up, made choices of their own. Worse, I discovered the hard way that no matter how hard I worked, no matter how determined I was to be the best mom I could be, I still came up short. I lost my patience. Snapped curt replies. Chose selfishness over serving. Not all the time and not every day, but enough to be fully aware of the fact that I was a flawed and less than perfect mom.

Yes, I knew the imperfection hidden behind the Photoshopped smiles in our fireplace frame, even if no one else could see. After cancer, those flaws became more apparent, highlighted by my desperation to do right by the ones I loved. I felt wave after wave of regret, seeing with painful clarity the many ways I hadn't been the mom I wanted to be.

As I stood in front of a filled church sanctuary on Mother's Day, taking in the faces of other equally human and struggling people, I knew the truth after cancer and all those months of wrestling: motherhood is more than posed and frameable moments.

It's not the sum of blissful images filling the pages of a scrapbook. A mother is made in the difficult, challenging, and very real crises that never make it to a page. It's choosing to love when you'd rather run away. Being a mother is becoming an expert at saying, "I'm sorry," "I forgive you," and "I love you," as many times as necessary. And teaching your children to do the same.

Motherhood didn't turn out quite like I'd thought, I told my new friends at DeWitt Community Church. It involved more hard work and less glamour than I'd dreamed once upon a time. We are a family who came together as a result of horrible loss. There is no way to erase this truth or ignore it. Divorce is the circumstance that brought us all together. Thrown together into swirling teacups, we tried to blend and recreate the magic of all we'd lost.

Although isolated by grief, we also learned to be joined by it. Divorce and remarriage are characters in our family's story, as is cancer. But they don't define us. Now, when I look at the family portrait on the mantel, I no longer see flaws and the many ways I failed.

I see a story taking shape behind the scenes.

Months before Syracuse, Troy called me to the kitchen late one night as I pulled out my pajamas and dressed for bed upstairs.

"Honey, can you come downstairs for a minute?"

The day had been a long one, and all I wanted to do was to crawl into bed and go to sleep. Couldn't this wait for tomorrow?

He called me a second time, kind but persistent. More than a little frustrated, I slid into my slippers and headed back down the stairs. I didn't expect what waited for me when I turned the corner and entered the kitchen.

Troy stood near the sink, and all three of our boys sat on barstools nearby. Even Tyler. Six months after he'd left, he'd come back home. Apologetic, ready to rebuild and reconcile with our family. Even so, the relationship remained strained for a time.

"What's wrong?" I braced myself for the worst. Why else would my husband and sons circle up late at night in the kitchen?

"Have a seat," Troy said. I obeyed. Then he turned to the boys. "I wrote a letter to Michele. I'm going to read it to her, but I want you to hear it too."

I didn't expect that. He unfolded two pages of lined paper, and from my place on a stool, I could see his handwriting filled the lines with blue ink. Quite possibly the most words he'd ever written. Troy didn't do things like this. Ever.

What followed in the next couple of minutes were some of the sweetest words of affirmation I've ever received to this day. But the biggest gift came after the letter was finished.

"Boys, I just told my wife a few of the things I love about her. Now it's your turn. I want you to tell her one thing you love about her. One thing, that's it."

I swallowed the lump in my throat. My teenage boys didn't do this. They didn't express emotion or affirmation except in grunt form. Would they resent him for asking? Would they even be able to do it?

I didn't have to wait to find out. Without a second's hesitation, Tyler spoke up. The oldest. The son who ousted me at Disneyland. The one who walked away from our family when he was sixteen years old. The son I'd loved as my own but feared he'd never love me in return.

He smiled. "I know she'll always love us. No matter what."

Have mercy.

In all of my mothering failings, I'd managed to get one thing right. Love. And it mattered most of all.

CHAPTER 11

The Ford and the Phone Call

We must be ready to allow ourselves to be interrupted by God.

—DIETRICH BONHOEFFER, *Life Together*

WHEN TROY AND I PASSED THE TEN-YEAR MARK OF MARRIAGE without shipping the other (or a child) to a barren arctic wilderness, we ran toward the next phase of our lives like a cat escaping a fire.

Thank God! I think we're gonna make it!

By some miracle, we'd defied the odds, made a second marriage work. As a reward, our long-awaited honeymoon phase perched on the other side of our parenting.

Something our friends called "empty nest."

Now, there was a time I thought empty nest a barren wasteland for washed-up parents. I loved being a mother more than anything else, couldn't imagine my days without the noise and activity of my boys. Did life exist postparenting? No longer of any use, parents of grown children were relegated to assisted-care facilities, bridge-playing collectives, and Denny's early-bird specials. Without children to feed, clothe, drive, and boss around, what in the world would I do with myself?

Then adolescence hit. One, two, three boys, one right after the other. *Ka-pow!* And suddenly Troy and I knew exactly what we'd do with ourselves postparenting.

Whatever we wanted.

So we gave "empty nest" a more appropriate title.

The Promised Land.

(Insert the "Hallelujah Chorus" here.)

Of course, launching our children into adulthood wasn't all parties and balloons. My heart hadn't grown *completely* cold and calloused. When Tyler graduated from high school, the year before cancer, I cried. Not a sweet, tender, "isn't she precious?" cry. The sloppy, drippy, hyperventilating kind. For weeks before his graduation day, I stayed up until the early hours of morning pulling together pictures and memories for his school-years scrapbook. With each page, each picture and memory, I felt our family changing in radical and unalterable ways. Time wouldn't be stopped. No more weekend camping trips. No more bedtime tuck-ins. No more pumpkin carving, Easter-egg hunting, and after-school cookie dunking.

I mourned how quickly those little-boy years passed. One moment, it seemed like parenting would never end. The next moment, it was gone. And in spite of all the difficulties, I wanted it back. I thought of all the ways I'd squandered the time, griping over all the attitudes, sleepless nights, and unrelenting responsibilities. In the process, I missed some of the wonder of watching a child grow into a man.

Too late. By the time I realized what I'd had, Tyler was crossing the graduation stage, diploma in hand. The scrapbook of his childhood was done. I cried for a solid month.

Then, one year later and two weeks after Mother's Day in Syracuse, our second son graduated from high school. Ryan. The son who cost us countless late nights working on last-minute science projects. The son teachers adored but couldn't motivate. The son whose report card came with much fear and trembling. Not because he lacked the intelligence or ability. He simply had better things to do.

So when Ryan's graduation day came, neither grief, regret, nor sloppy-drippy crying made an appearance. Instead, joy.

Abundant, unrestrained, high-fiving joy.

Even so, tears would've been impossible to see. Instead, rain. Torrential downpours of it. It appeared God wept with joy at the prospect of our son's graduating from high school.

In spite of the weather, school administrators continued with the outdoor ceremony at Colorado's Red Rocks Amphitheatre. Parents, grandparents, brothers, sisters, and friends covered themselves as best they could with ponchos, hats, blankets, and umbrellas, all of which proved futile while sitting in an open-air venue in a flood of near-biblical proportions.

Most spectators left, unable to endure the elements to experience the entire graduation. The longer the ceremony continued, the sparser the crowd.

Not us. No way. It had taken no small effort to get to this day. Like running a marathon and nearing the end, we weren't leaving until we heard Ryan's name announced over the loudspeakers. That was our finish line, when we knew administrators and teachers couldn't change their minds.

I'll never forget his moment on the stage. To secure proof, we snapped picture after picture with rain-smeared lenses as he approached teachers and principal.

Then it happened. His name over the loudspeaker.

"Ryan Cushatt!"

Cheers, whistles, and all sorts of raucous celebration erupted from the right middle bleacher seats, where a dad, stepmom, two brothers, and three grandparents jointly held their breath.

We hugged and high-fived for a solid minute, grinning like children at Christmas.

Finally.

Finally.

Later, I turned to my husband, nudged him in the ribs. "Congratulations, honey." I laughed. "You graduated."

~

With Ryan graduated, our family now consisted of two boys post–high school and a third about to drive. The Promised Land was within reach. Peaceful, abundant, freedom-filled territory. I could almost taste the milk and honey.

Within the week, Troy and I started dreaming of the second half of our lives. Imagining how we'd spend days and nights without demanding, hormone-fluctuating adolescent dictators ruling our household.

Quiet sunset dinners on the deck.

Early bedtimes in a silent (and clean) house.

Saturday morning sleep-ins followed by breakfast in bed.

A clean car without Gatorade on the upholstery and boogers on the windows.

Yes, ma'am. The possibilities were endless. Glory hallelujah.

Our first order of business was to sell our eight-passenger Ford Expedition: the Big Blue Beast. This I celebrated with great exultation. We'd bought it months after our wedding, the means to drive our three boys and their friends to soccer practices and school. It made sense, when gas was still less than two dollars a gallon.

But I had a love-hate relationship with that SUV. It served our family well for ten years, didn't break down or cause us any problems. But for a solid decade, I got nine miles to a gallon and spent the annual budget of a small country to fill it up.

And I never could figure out how to park the ridiculous thing.

Now, with two of our boys driving, we no longer needed the Big Blue Beast. In front of our house sat a virtual parking lot of used teenage cars. We no longer needed the eight seats to transport a posse of boys to practice or youth group or school. Instead, we could downsize to something smaller with better gas mileage. Something easier to park.

We found it soon after we started shopping. Used, yes. But the previous owner had been a young, single woman. Sans children. Let me say that again, *no children*.

A cute, four-passenger, smoky-gray Volvo S40. Leather seats. Tinted windows. CD player. Moon roof. Twenty-five miles to the gallon. Not a booger in sight.

Milk and honey, baby. Milk and honey.

I fell in love with that car. Drove it all over Denver, windows down, music up, with all the sass of a high school girl on the pom squad. With the purchase of that adorable car, I transformed from a washed-up mama looking at assisted-living options into an energetic, middle-aged maven ready to paint the town.

Empty nest, we're on our way!

I drove that car for three weeks.

Three weeks.

Then. July 19. Exactly two months to the day after Ryan's rain-soaked graduation day.

When the phone rang.

Again.

~

A second phone call.

Eight months, several surgeries, and countless doctor's appointments after the first.

You'd think I would've been more prepared this time, ready for the ringing phone to rip through the landscape of my life. But this call brought as much surprise as the first. Perhaps more.

Midafternoon, I sat at home, alone. Twelve days before, I'd had another surgery. A water bottle sat close by, the cold liquid the only real relief to the constant mouth pain.

I felt the phone vibrate on the sofa next to me.

Troy Cushatt.

A glance at the screen identified my husband as the caller. I picked up. As I'd done hundreds of times before.

He started with "Hi" and ended less than a minute later with "So, what do you think?" In between these ordinary words he said words that would change us—change me—forever.

A woman needed our help, a mom who could no longer care for her three small children. Twin four-year-olds and a five-year-old. Crumbling under addiction, she couldn't be a mom anymore, couldn't even take care of herself. By some miracle, after years of struggle and resistance, she finally asked for help, for someone to give her children a home, food, love. And put their broken pieces back together again.

Us.

I held my breath, thinking, trying to hold an ocean of reality in too-small hands. This was the mother of all decisions, a life-hinging moment that would change every detail of our day-to-day. We knew this, even as Troy and I talked in rushed, staccato half-sentences on the phone. But we had no idea how much would change, what we'd gain but also what we'd lose in the gaining.

"Will you take them?" the mother had asked.

I wanted to scream, "No! Are you out of your mind?!"

That's the honest truth of it. Parenting hadn't been a picnic the first time around. Good, rewarding, but anything but easy. Although I'd spent a lifetime dreaming of motherhood, reality turned out to be far more work and far less dreamlike. Perhaps that was the adolescence talking. We were still neck deep in the teenage years, dealing with all the chaos and conflict that come with living in a house full of hormonal boys. There was always someone vying for control, someone trying to assert his independence and strong-arm the grown-ups to the ground. It was exhausting, this parenting gig.

Besides, I was eight months postcancer with zero guarantees about my future. Was it wise to take on such a responsibility? Was I physically able to do this thing, keep up with the needs of small children, when speaking continued to be a challenge? What about my boys? They'd already been through a rough year. Would they think we were crazy?

Were we?

We neared the end of our parenting marathon, bodies dehydrated and muscles weak. Only the sight of the finish line kept us pushing forward. "Just get through," a family expert advised over radio waves. "Adolescence is tough, but just get through it." We'd abandoned our expectations and settled for survival.

And now someone was asking us to roll up sweaty sleeves and dig in one more time. For three children who would need even more than the first three. A mile from our finish line, we faced a choice. Run through to the end without looking left or right, front or back. Don't allow for distractions or interruptions. Follow the course, finish the race. Be done with it, as planned.

Or.

Or.

Loop back around and run the whole race again. Another 26.2 miles. On legs that have already wearied of the run.

"Will you take them?" she'd asked.

Scratch that. God asked, in a voice I'd grown to love even more over the prior eight months. Not audible, like my husband's baritone or sixteen-year-old's tenor. Instead, an urge I knew wasn't rooted in my own emotion. An otherworldly whisper to risk, to trust.

At that moment, I no longer saw a finish line, no longer felt the ache in my legs or sweat on my brow. Instead, I saw three small children with nowhere else to go. No more, no less.

"Yes," I said. "Let's do it. We'll take these kids. No question."

With those words, our second honeymoon ended as quickly as the first.

And we started shopping for another eight-passenger car.

PART 2

Death and Life

CHAPTER 12

Popsicles, the Park, and Jesus

It is not objective proof of God's existence that we want but, whether we use religious language for it or not, the experience of God's presence. That is the miracle that we are really after.

—FREDERICK BUECHNER, *The Magnificent Defeat*

A SINGLE SUITCASE.

Child size. Maybe two feet across, less than a foot deep. Worn and frayed around the edges with a zipper barely holding things together.

Inside, folded, sat the belongings of three children. Years of life packed into a two-by-one-foot space. A few shorts, skirts, and shirts. A handful of socks and underpants. Three light jackets. Pajamas.

The owners of the suitcase—children—stood in the Walmart parking lot, between the car that brought them and the car that would take them away. The oldest, five-year-old Princess, stood shy and quiet, a little lady with long blond hair and the bluest of blue eyes. Jack and Peanut, four-year-old twins, a boy and a girl, stayed close to each other. They looked small, too small.

Each gripped a blanket, the only scrap of familiarity in a world of unknowns. Eyes round and hollow, they looked at us.

I knelt down, meeting their anxiety with my own.

"Hi there." I touched the smallest girl's arm, tried to mask my trembling with both warmth and enthusiasm. "Do you remember who we are?"

Two months before, we'd played together at a family wedding. At the time, we had no idea how important those brief moments of connection would be. In a Walmart parking lot on a Thursday in July, it made all the difference in the world.

Heads nodded and mouth corners turned up in the first hint of a smile.

They remembered. Thank God, they remembered. We weren't strangers. We were the grown-ups who tickled and made them giggle over large slices of wedding cake and cups of fruit punch. The fear in their eyes faded, just a bit. I'm guessing it did the same in my own.

Troy transferred their suitcase into the trunk of our tiny gray car, and I grabbed two small bags of toys. Everything they owned.

"Mommy's sick," the five-year-old blurted, assuming leadership of the three. "We're staying with you until she gets better."

I turned, surprised. She knew, at least in part, the reason for the suitcase. She searched my face for confirmation. I didn't know what to say.

"That's right." I offered my best smile. "We're going to take good care of you while Mommy gets better, okay?"

I wanted her to believe it, to know that I would love her like she longed to be loved. That she would be safe and protected, hugged and held, as long as necessary. The emptiness in her eyes told me she didn't buy it.

After one last goodbye to Grandma, we buckled three car

seats and children into the back of our empty-nest car. I snapped my seat belt. Troy put the key in the ignition and pulled out of the Walmart parking lot and onto Interstate 25. With a final backward glance, I turned forward and looked up ahead.

"Let's go home."

~

There are three phases of parenting to which most moms and dads never want to return:

Two-hour feedings.

Diaper bags.

And car seats.

As Troy and I drove back to Denver, Colorado, with three children in tow, we privately high-fived the fact that we'd escaped the first two.

But, God help us, car seats. Three of them. For four more years. With tiny little bottoms filling each one.

Oh wow, oh wow, oh wow.

My brain couldn't wrap itself around this new reality. So I kept looking over my shoulder into the previously untried back seat of my car.

Yep. Still there. Three little people, going home with us.

I grabbed Troy's free hand, glanced into the back seat again. One drew pictures in the fog on the windows with her fingers. Two others drank Bug Juice out of bottles, a sweet treat Grandma picked up before the drop-off. It was just a matter of time before cherry red and raspberry blue spilled on the unstained floor.

Fifteen minutes in and the empty-nest car was about to be initiated into parenting.

We're back in the races, baby.

An hour later, maybe more, we pulled into our driveway.

"Is this your house?" Princess, the five-year-old, asked as Troy put the car in park and turned off the engine.

"Yes, it is. It's your house now too." We sat there for an extra second, breathing, before unlocking the doors.

Troy unloaded the suitcase while I led the way into our house. A couple of feet inside the door, our black Labrador retriever, Nika, covered all three in sloppy wet dog kisses. I panicked for a second, not knowing how dog and children would get along. In seconds, gasps gave way to giggles. Who knew? A dog's slobbery affection eased the initial transition better than any of our words.

Pooch-to-preschooler introductions made, the children walked through our foyer wide-eyed. Cathedral ceilings, wrought-iron railings, bookshelves, leather couch, travertine-tiled bathrooms. Although familiar and ordinary to us, it appeared mansionlike to three children who'd never really had a home. From what we could tell, they hadn't lived in the same place—or slept in the same bed—for much longer than a few months at a time since birth.

Watching them tour our home changed how I saw it. Three years before, we'd bought this fixer-upper as an investment. A general contractor, Troy turned the outdated, neglected home into something model-quality. Twice the size of our prior house, it had more bedrooms, baths, and square footage than we needed. And with Troy's professional touch, it now had granite countertops, maple floors, stone fireplaces, and countless other custom additions.

Most days, I felt guilty about living in such a home. We planned to flip it, move into something smaller and farther out of town, once Troy finished the updates and our youngest, Jacob, graduated from high school. It felt too nice, too vast for an ordinary family like ours.

But then a phone call that came with three children. As I led these little ones to their bedrooms, as I watched their faces light up with gratefulness, I no longer saw a too-big house.

Instead, I saw providence.

You saw it coming, didn't you? You knew.

The fact that he did, that the God who loved these children more than I could imagine had been working behind the scenes all along, braced me for all the upheaval and unknowns yet to come.

For the first half hour, they explored every room. The bathroom with the tall stone sink. The living room with the glossy-black baby grand piano. The bedroom with the giant sleigh bed where the grown-ups slept. When they'd seen every inch of the inside, they moved to the back yard. And there discovered the trampoline that had entertained our boys for years.

They spent most of the next five days right there, warmed by the summer sun while jumping up and down. I don't remember much else about those first hours and days. It's a blur. Perhaps a result of time passed. Or, more likely, too much for a brain and heart to take in at once. Instead of details, I remember images, overpowering sights, smells, and sounds that evidenced a life turned on end.

Baby blankets in the laundry basket.

Tiny shoes scattered by the front door.

Coloring books on the kitchen table.

Three children wide awake and ready to play at 5:00 a.m.

No doubt about it, the Cushatt family wasn't the same. All it took was a short drive to make my home almost unrecognizable. We still had the sights and sounds of our teenage boys. The mood swings, slamming doors, and sound of the refrigerator opening and closing, opening and closing. But layered over the top of the familiar now lay the unfamiliar. New and unknown experiences around which I hadn't yet wrapped my head.

So while they jumped on our trampoline, wrestled with our boys, and explored every corner of our home, I watched. Tried to uncover clues about what our life was going to look like from that day forward.

Maybe it was wishful thinking on my part, my impossible tendency to hope when evidence tells me not to. Or maybe it was simply the calm before the storm. But every smile and laugh convinced me that maybe we'd been mistaken. Maybe the trauma that marked their short history hadn't left any scars. They appeared ordinary children, playful and happy. Perhaps they hadn't been affected by their past?

Now, months and years later, I see the clues I missed—or didn't want to see—those first few days.

The hollowness of their eyes, and the dark circles underneath. Even when laughing, the emotion didn't seem to make it to their eyes.

Their dull, thin, patchy hair. Evidence of malnutrition.

The way they shoveled second and third helpings of dinner and swallowed without chewing.

The absence of tears when many should've been shed. Children who said goodbye to their mother hours before should cry, shouldn't they?

I didn't want to see these things. Didn't want to grapple with the massive brokenness that came along with their two-by-one suitcase. Call it arrogance or ignorance, but I believed I could wash and wipe away all the wrong that had been done. I wanted to believe any loss replaceable, every wound healable.

So I dumped blankets and the contents of the suitcase into my washing machine.

I bought tearless shampoo and yummy-smelling soap to scrub their skin clean of the smell and grime.

I made double boxes of macaroni and cheese and dished it up in heaping portions.

And I served up cookies and popsicles on the back porch, where we licked fingers and laughed and pretended everything was fine.

~

"How about we walk to the park? After dinner?"

It'd been a particularly long day. Four solid days of adjusting to an unrecognizable life, and I was exhausted. Preschoolers are cute and precious and cheek-pinching adorable when they belong to someone else. They're life-suckers when you have one foot in middle age and you live with three of them.

Cheers erupted from the little people sitting at the kitchen counter. For ten glorious seconds, I was the best mom in the world. Which, after raising teenagers, was the longest I'd held that title in more than five years. As I finished cleaning up the mountain of dinner dishes, I could barely muster the energy for a smile. The littles, on the other hand, started bouncing up and down around our house like a pondful of frogs.

I'm not sure how I managed to get them to sit still long enough to pack six feet into six tiny little tennis shoes and tie them in beautiful double-knots. After I finished, sweat dripped in dark places.

Note to self: Teach Shoe-Tying 101. ASAP.

It took us twenty minutes to get to the park with three pairs of itty-bitty legs. When we crested the hill to see the wooden outline of swings and jungle gyms and slides, they took off running. *Wheeeeeee!* times three.

Jack settled into a sand shovel and tried to figure out how to dig. Princess went right for the swings. Peanut started climbing as high as her little legs could go.

I'd forgotten how much children love parks. How much I loved them. As it turned out, I'd forgotten quite a bit about parenting small children.

That happens. Over time, as children grow and fully inhabit the next phase of childhood, we forget the yesterdays. Except for a scrapbook filled with photos or a journal packed with notes, the vast majority of our experiences evaporate like morning mist when faced with the sun.

As I watched them swing and slide and chase each other around the playground, I wondered if it was wise to go back. If it was even possible.

Could we do this thing? I'm not talking on paper or in conversation. But really do this thing. In real life. For years and years.

It's one thing to say, "Yes, let's do it," over a five-minute phone call. It's an entirely different thing to wake up at 5:00 a.m. day after day, without end or reprieve.

Could we do it? Could I? Honestly, I didn't know. In many ways, those first several days passed like scenes pulled from a movie. Loss and rescue, grief and joy. With a heart aching to deliver a childhood to children who'd nearly lost it, I dove into my role with passion and purpose.

Here I come to save the day!

I'm a sucker for a good story. Still, even with all the picturesque movielike drama, reality was anything but easy. In fact, it was difficult and draining enough to give both Troy and me pause. We'd done a week. I had no doubt we could tackle a month, maybe two or three.

But to raise three more small children? To start over and carry it through for as long as needed? That's a lot to ask of anyone.

The idealistic side of me wanted to be a hero. The realistic side of me wanted to take a nap. And, sitting in the park watching three littles buzz around without any sign of slowing, the realistic voice seemed to be louder at the moment than the other. I'm far less noble than I'd like to be.

I watched the sun set over the Rocky Mountains; tension burned in my heart. I raked a hand through my hair as I watched seemingly ordinary children playing in the neighborhood park. Only I knew, deep down, ordinary was a mirage.

Breathe, Michele. Don't tackle a lifetime of unknowns in a few minutes at the park. Instead, play. Laugh. Tomorrow will come soon enough.

With that, I rose from my railroad-tie bench and headed for the swings.

"How about a push?"

"Me! Me! Push meeeee!" Princess squealed her delight, grabbing for any scrap of attention I could offer. She didn't yet know how to pump legs, go higher. I would have to help her fly.

"Wheeeeee!"

Her sister joined us. "Higher! Higher!"

Soon the sun finished its descent over the mountains, painting us a miraculous display.

"Look at that!" I pointed to the west. I didn't want them to miss the oranges and pinks and purples coloring the sky. A sunset like that demanded appreciation, acknowledgment. "Beautiful, isn't it?"

Princess and Peanut jumped off the swings as Jack finished his final slide and raced to join us. We left the park behind and walked down the path that turned toward home, a quiet hush settling over all of us.

Princess slipped her hand in mine.

"How does the sky do that?" she asked.

I looked at her face, alight with the sunset's fire, turning her cheeks a deeper shade of pink.

"What do you mean? Turn pink and purple and orange?"

She nodded, waiting for me to give her the secrets of the universe.

"God does it. He paints the sky because he loves nothing more than giving us beautiful gifts." It *was* beautiful, and definitely a gift. One of the summer's best.

"Who's God?"

What? Her question shook me. I didn't expect it, had no idea how she'd lived five years—1,825 days—without hearing about the one who loved her most of all.

But what to say? How did I explain the God I've always known to a little girl who'd never heard of him before?

I squeezed her hand. "He's the one who made you, sweet girl. The one who gave you arms and legs and your beautiful blue eyes." I smiled, winked. Maybe it was the lingering light of the descending sun, but she seemed to blush at the reference.

"God is the one who paints the sky. To let us know he sees us—you, your brother and sister. And me. It's his way of letting us know how much he loves us."

It wasn't much, but it was a beginning. A single conversation to let them know that beyond the chaos of their circumstances, beyond the losses and grief and unknowns, there was a God who was big enough to paint masterpieces in the sky. To figure out the future and make sure they felt at home, wherever they were.

And for the moment, it was enough for me too.

CHAPTER 13

Counting the Cost

The ultimate measure of a man is not where he stands in moments of comfort and convenience, but where he stands in times of challenge and controversy. The true neighbor will risk his position, his prestige, and even his life for the welfare of others.

—M. L. KING JR., *Strength to Love*

Ministry that costs nothing accomplishes nothing.

—J. H. JOWETT, *The Preacher, His Life and Work*

I WENT ON MY FIRST MISSION TRIP JUST DAYS AFTER MY SIXTEENTH birthday. But my transformation began a year earlier.

At a Christ in Youth Conference in Adrian, Michigan, against my better judgment, I walked down an aisle during an altar call. I wasn't an altar-call junkie, one of those girls who rededicated every time a tear made an appearance. I typically avoided anything that made me stand out, appear different or (God forbid) a spectacle.

Until my legs practically sprinted to the front to the tune of "I Surrender All."

I can't tell you what the speaker had said moments before,

the theme of the week, or what thoughts were spinning in my crazy head. But something happened that night. It wasn't a radical transformation or an instantaneous awakening. But a spark of something real and true came to hot life within. I wanted my living to be about more than boy trouble, girl drama, and fingernail polish. In a moment, I felt a warm awareness of a big, wide world outside of myself, a world filled with faces and stories unknown to me but seen and treasured by the God of us all. I knew some lived in gross poverty, needing food and water. Others were desperate for words of peace or hope. And I could be the one to give such words to them.

I couldn't stay in my seat, even if I'd wanted to.

So there, in front of several hundred students and adults, I allowed myself to be pulled to the front by a burning and unidentifiable ache. With friends and strangers as witnesses, I committed to a life of serving Jesus. I'd known him my whole life, been baptized as a Christian when I was seven. But now I wanted to make my whole life about him, to "do his work." Of course, I didn't have a clue what that meant. But like any self-respecting teenage girl, I hoped it involved something glamorous and wild. Maybe Africa.

The next August, right after my sixteenth birthday, I flew to the Dominican Republic for my first mission trip. Not exactly Africa, but a big step from my ho-hum midwestern hometown. Over the course of seventeen days, we built a church foundation, taught VBS, played with children, and told those searching about Jesus. All the while, we ate a ridiculous amount of plantains—raw, boiled, baked, fried, mashed. And, in spite of the plantains, my heart spark for missions burned ever brighter.

This was my purpose, my life's work.

I'll go anywhere, do anything. I'm yours, God!

Those were my words. And I meant every one of them, as much as a hormonally hijacked girl can.

I carried my promise with me into adulthood, through college, nursing school, and all those complicated years of marriage and mothering. As it turned out, Troy's heart carried a similar ache, felt the same calling. Which is why a year before the littles came, we planned to travel to Haiti the last week of July.

Mission work had become a part of our family experience, something we did along with our boys. Even before cancer, we'd committed to this Haiti trip along with our youngest son, to repair and rebuild a dilapidated building in northern Haiti, convert it into a medical clinic the village desperately needed. I'd been the team lead and organizer, Troy the construction expertise. Several teenagers and adults were set to go with us.

Then, in a strange twist of timing, the phone rang and three littles moved into our home a week before our departure. We felt torn. Two gaping needs, worlds apart. Eight people (not to mention an entire Haitian village) counted on our leadership and trusted us to follow through. But the littles needed us too. They needed the stability of a mom and dad who loved them. What were we to do?

To our relief, a relative stepped up and offered to help the week we were gone, someone the littles knew and with whom they felt safe. And so we said goodbye almost as quickly as we said hello. And I repacked the two-by-one suitcase a week after we brought the littles home.

It wasn't easy, getting on that plane. In less than a week, my heart had already grown like a vine around theirs. At the same time, six days with three preschoolers felt like a month. Maybe longer. Sweet and unparalleled? Absolutely. But I-could-sleep-for-the-rest-of-my-life exhausting as well.

I confess, in many ways our escape to Haiti came at a good time. An escape to Hawaii would've been better, but Haiti worked. Troy shared my reservations, although his concerns circled around my ongoing health issues more than anything else. It'd been less than three weeks since the last surgery. Dropping three special-needs children into the middle of my healing hadn't worked out so well. The added talking and activity brought on more pain and swelling. Again I couldn't communicate or eat without difficulty.

Not to mention the whole cyst ridiculousness. It was still too early to know whether the last procedure had been successful. The cyst could still come back. If it did, I'd need another surgery, maybe another, until it resolved. No one knew when the whole frustrating mess would be wrapped up and put away for good. If ever.

Sobered by our parenting-preschoolers reality check, needing to slow down and think, Troy and I decided to take advantage of our Haiti trip to pray, process, and make some kind of permanent decision—for me, our family, and for these three littles who longed for a place to call home. We needed to see beyond the fluff and fantasy to face the rock-hard truth: this was a fourteen-year commitment.

Not a weekend romp or a weeklong vacation with someone else's kids. This was choosing to parent three children to adulthood. A radical, earth-shattering, no-turning-back decision. We needed to be sure. And absolutely ready.

Only later would we see the irony of taking a mission trip when the most pressing mission waited for us back at home.

~

Haiti.

It's difficult to describe Haiti to someone who has never been. The rotting garbage. The open-air markets with vendors selling raw chicken and goat heads sweltering in the sun for hours. The constant stench of sewage mingled with burnt trash, sticking to our clothes, skin, and suitcases. The shoeless children and blank-eyed mothers walking as zombies through the day's tasks.

The smells surprised me most, overpowering the moment the airplane doors swung open. As we traveled by open-air bus through Port-au-Prince's city streets, it only got worse. It took a full day to adjust to the smells, although I never did get used to it. It was all I could do not to cover my nose with a T-shirt from home that still carried the faint scent of detergent and fabric softener.

Two days after arriving in Port-au-Prince, on the day of my fortieth birthday, our host, Greg, of Christian World Outreach, rented an air-conditioned van to transport us and all our gear to LaJeune, the job site. Even by American standards, the van was nice. By Haitian standards, it was an unheard of luxury. Considering the ninety-degree heat, I thought it an appropriate birthday gift.

Greg said the drive to our job site would take four hours, give or take. Which is why I didn't know what to think when, two hours later, we pulled to a stop in Hinche.

"Go ahead and unload. All of it," Greg said, referring to our duffels and crates of supplies.

I didn't understand. Why unload when we hadn't yet arrived at LaJeune? According to the clock, we still had another two hours and miles to go.

We unloaded anyway, trusting our leader. Then, several minutes later, surrounded by our piles of gear, I watched our beautiful air-conditioned van and its driver turn around and head back to Port-au-Prince.

Uh-oh.

Enter a tiny white pickup truck. With hanging bumper, ripped canvas cover, and a see-through floorboard beneath the back seat.

A mistake. It had to be a mistake.

"Where's our truck? The one taking us to LaJeune?" I asked Greg.

He laughed.

"Load up!" Greg smiled, clearly enjoying himself.

An hour later, we took off. Four of us squeezed inside the double cab of the white pickup with a Creole-speaking driver, bags on our laps, bodies squished together like sardines. The other six members of our group sat in the truck bed, on benches or hanging off the gate, legs dangling off the back bumper.

If only the Department of Transportation could see us now.

It took less than ten minutes for me to understand the vehicle change. A mile ahead, the paved road gave way to dirt. Not a flat, hard-packed dirt road, like we see in rural American towns. But the kind washed out by monsoonal rains a dozen times over.

For two hours, we moved at a slower-than-a-school-zone pace, navigating long stretches of mud and standing water deep enough to cover ankles and shins, and weaving in and out of boulder fields.

Now I understood. A shiny, air-conditioned van wouldn't have made this trip. Only a beat-up pickup could navigate this kind of road.

Pop!

A loud noise made every one of us jump. The driver stopped, turned off the engine, and climbed out. Through the open windows, I heard a long string of Creole. In spite of four years of French, I couldn't understand a single word. It didn't sound good.

A broken axle, Greg told us. Our driver would try to fix it.

Fix it? I know next to nothing about cars, but I was pretty sure a snapped axle wasn't duct-tapable. Especially in middle-of-nowhere Haiti. Definitely not good. We had work to do, and we needed to get to it.

For the second time that day, we unloaded and waited. Finding a small patch of shade underneath a tree, we stood at a distance and watched our driver work. A fine way to spend my fortieth birthday, I thought, sweating like a glass of iced tea in the heat of summer. But without a drop of iced tea to be found. It was a waste of time, trying to fix a broken axle. Impossible. We might as well turn around and go back.

The driver seemed undeterred. Focused, he didn't look at us or say a word.

I don't know how long we stood there. Forty minutes, maybe an hour. Then another string of Creole.

"Okay, load up." Greg announced. "It's fixed."

Fixed? Not possible!

Turns out our Creole-speaking driver packed a spare. *A spare axle*. God bless him.

Before he ever met us, our driver prepared to meet a need. Then, when the opportunity presented itself, he got to work and made it happen. Without complaint about the inconvenience. He simply saw a need and met it, the best way he knew how.

Three years before our Haiti trip, in the middle of 2008, I witnessed the exact opposite. On another mission trip, this time to South Africa, Troy and I worked in a squatters' camp of sixty thousand of the poorest of South Africa's poor, a village called Intabazwe.

Ironically, sitting just below this squatters' camp and within eyesight, sat Harrismith, a small town that looked as if it'd been plucked right out of the heart of Iowa. A main street complete with grocery store, restaurant, park, and paved streets. And, off the thoroughfare, long lines of houses, with front doors and windows and full refrigerators inside.

Intabazwe and Harrismith. Wealth and poverty living as neighbors. Close enough to touch, but rarely doing so. As I spent my days in filth looking down on the fine, the contrast stirred up questions I couldn't answer. How did the hungry live so close to food-stocked kitchens without resentment destroying their souls? And how did homeowners and restaurant-goers sit at tables, forking steak into their mouths, without the food lodging in their throats? Did they see the starving on the other side of their doors?

The dichotomy convicted me, like a knife slicing at my selfishness until I dared to let myself bleed. I didn't want to be that person, the woman sitting so comfortable in her air-conditioned home with doors locked, windows closed, and full refrigerator hoarding a stash of food. I didn't want to live blind to the hungry beyond my front door.

I discovered Isaiah 58:10 while in South Africa, later tattooed it on my ankle and then carried it again with me to Haiti. "If you spend yourselves in behalf of the hungry and satisfy the needs of the oppressed, then your light will rise in the darkness, and your night will become like the noonday."[18]

Want a life rich with joy? Spend yourself. Desire fullness from head to toe? Find someone to feed. Looking for a life that shines, turns dark into light? Find a need and meet it. No questions asked.

Not all that different from a Haitian driver who spent a half day and a spare axle to get us where we needed to go.

In both Haiti and Africa, I learned a lesson I needed to bring back home, a lesson that would fuel our decision and attitude about three small children. More than twenty years before, on a long walk down an aisle at a youth conference and to the words of "I Surrender All," I'd made big, grandiose promises to God.

I'll go anywhere, God! Do anything for you!

I thought that meant assuming a missionary's life, using vacation time for short-term mission trips, and serving a world outside of my door. Then when our boys turned adult and started their own lives, Troy and I planned to make our promise permanent. We'd sell our home, cars, and furniture, and move where God sent us. Haiti, perhaps. Maybe Africa. That was our plan. To go wherever, whenever.

I now know God heard my promises, both my childlike pronouncements and adultlike offerings. Then, years later, when I thought I knew what he had in mind, he spoke back, interrupted my plotting and planning with a single phone call and three children.

You promised to go anywhere, do anything, Michele. Sell everything and serve me on the mission field.

Yes, true. I'd said that more times than I could count.

I'm bringing the mission field to you. Are you still game?

I'll never forget that day, the way God turned my food-laden tables and forced me to see the fulfillment of my promise in a way I hadn't planned or expected.

God wasn't asking me to *go*. He was asking me to *stay*.

To leave Haiti and return to my four-bedroom, air-conditioned house. To open my home and see three hungry children right outside my front door.

I wanted to renegotiate. *Send me to Africa! Mars! Anywhere but here!*

The truth was a mission trip would be easier. Even then I knew that, after only a week playing house with preschoolers. It'd be easier to pack a suitcase, go on a short-term adventure, and return home a week or two later to wash the dirt out of my clothes, put the suitcase in the closet, and log my memories in a scrapbook. A worthy act of service? Yes, of course. But neatly packaged and not too interrupting. A mission trip would allow me to keep my grandiose promises to manageable portions, something that didn't stretch and sting to the point of sacrifice.

Instead, God asked me to step out of my shiny, air-conditioned life and climb into something less comfortable. It wasn't glamorous or wild. It wouldn't earn me more stamps in my passport or exotic pictures for display. And quite honestly, it didn't look all that much fun.

But the life of a true Jesus-follower—someone who both says and means her promise of "anywhere" and "anything"—doesn't follow smooth, paved roads. And a comfortable, air-conditioned van isn't going to get her where he wants her to go.

Jesus said, "Whoever wants to be my disciple must deny themselves and take up their cross and follow me. For whoever wants to save their life will lose it, but whoever loses their life for me and for the gospel will save it."[19]

The only way to find the life I always wanted was to let the lesser life go.

To see a need and drop everything to meet it. Without complaint, second-guessing, or contemplation of the cost.

It would cost far more than I ever imagined.

CHAPTER 14

Love in the Land of Limbo

[Daddy] said, "All children must look after their own upbringing." Parents can only give good advice or put them on the right paths, but the final forming of a person's character lies in their own hands.

—ANNE FRANK, *Anne Frank: The Diary of a Young Girl*

Not all who wander are lost.

—J. R. R. TOLKIEN, "All That Is Gold Does Not Glitter"

WE CAME BACK FROM HAITI WITH SLEEVES ROLLED UP, READY TO add three children to our family. Full of peace and confidence that God knew exactly what needed to happen. We simply needed to follow his lead, take one day at a time. Maybe breathe into a paper sack.

Then, again, about the time we thought we had it all figured out, the plot thickened.

The cyst came back.

I noticed a fullness, halfway through our trip to Haiti. I ignored it, tried to wish it away. But within a couple of days of our return stateside, after picking up our littles and diving back into life, it grew too big to ignore.

By now I knew the routine, regardless of how much I resented it. I called my surgeon, and she put yet another procedure on the books. August 16.

I responded to this fabulous news the only way any reasonable adult woman could: I bared my teeth and prepped to throw something. Then I cried, another one of those fist-pounding, sloppy cries. I was tired of other people's hands in my mouth. Weary of slow and painful recoveries. Sick of mashed-stinking-potatoes. It ticked me off.

My ranting changed nothing. I couldn't strong-arm my circumstances. My only choice? Move forward. Walk through it. Again, dang it.

But this new development caused bigger problems than more pain and mashed potatoes.

What were we going to do about the littles?

And the Cushatt family rollercoaster continued. It was a question we didn't immediately have an answer to. After surgery, I wouldn't be able to talk or eat normally for at least a couple of weeks. I knew from experience that rest and silence were the only path to healing. I could navigate recovery with teenagers, somewhat. But Troy and I knew it would be impossible with three high-needs four- and five-year-olds. How do you explain to little ones that Mommy can't talk? Worse, there was a good chance I'd need another surgery in six to eight weeks. Perhaps several others. At this point, there was no end in sight.

The kids deserved a stable home, and with my health in flux, we weren't sure we could give it to them. So we made a tough decision, one far more difficult than we realized. For a full week after we returned from Haiti, the littles stayed with us and we laughed and played and did our best to be an ordinary family. Then, on the afternoon of August 15, hours before my next surgery, we said goodbye. Again. With no small amount of heartbreak, we dropped them off with another relative. Indefinitely.

In three short weeks my heart had wrapped itself around the idea of becoming a mother again. I learned their favorite foods, their unique personalities, how they liked to spend quiet afternoons coloring. We shared Disney movies, bedtime tuck-ins, and Sunday mornings at church. Then, just that fast, they left. Yet another piece of my life robbed by cancer.

In the absence of their chatter, questions bounced like ping-pong balls in my head. Would my cyst go away this time? Would this be the last surgery? If so, would the doctor give me an all-clear? And if I got an all-clear, would we bring the children home for good?

Welcome to the Land of Limbo. As if I hadn't already set up house and laid out a doormat there.

Once again I found my planned and scheduled self in the middle of a messy unknown. No explanation or reassurances. No dates, calendar of events, or three-step plan. I knew I'd have surgery August 16. Beyond that I didn't have a clue.

I hated the limbo life. A strong word, but the right one. I heard friends talk about their boring and uneventful lives, and I envied their ordinary. We seemed to be bouncing from one crisis to another, without reprieve. I would've done anything for boring and ordinary.

But sometimes messy is the necessary beginning to the makings of extraordinary.

⁓

It'd become our summer ritual when our boys were little. Two parents, three boys, one giant pot of spaghetti with extra marinara.

And zero forks.

Once a summer, before boys became men, we ate a spaghetti feast in the back yard without utensils. A slimy, disgusting mess, I tell you. My boys ate it up.

Mannerless eating went against everything my mama and daddy taught me. Three hundred and sixty-four days of the year, I nagged with unceasing reminders about etiquette.

"Close your mouth while you chew."

"For crying out loud, your shirt is not a napkin."

"A pork chop is not bite-size. Try cutting it with that little thing on the right. It's called a *knife*."

Animals, I tell you. My boys are animals. Why I bothered to buy plates and silverware and display them on beautiful placemats I have no idea. I should've set out troughs. If you watched them eat dinner, you'd think they were raised by wolves. I can reassure you they had a mama and she taught them how to use both fork and napkin. They just didn't listen.

So once a summer, for a single meal, we allowed them to eat like they wanted to. Without a single manner within two square blocks. No forks or spoons. No napkins, fingers, or hands. Only a plate piled with noodles and red sauce, and a cherubic face primed to dive into the mess.

They loved it. No, really. *Loved it*. Once, Tyler got a canned pea stuck in his nose, marinara and Parmesan from hairline to chin. He grinned like a child at Christmas, and I couldn't resist capturing it for digital photographic eternity. I'm saving that baby for a more opportune time, say when he introduces us one day to his fiancee. Whoever she is, God bless her, she deserves to know.

I admit the Summer Spaghetti Palooza became a highlight

for the grown-ups as well. I was bit more shy about drowning my moisturized face in a pool of sauce. It's not easy for me to abandon manners for the mess. All I can see is the cleanup and postnasal drip on the other side. Still, I followed the no-manners rule and ate my noodles hands-free. Troy, unlike me, showed zero reservation. Seconds after his dinner-prayer amen, he entered the noodley pool like an Olympic diver.

Why do we do this? Why do civilized and respectable adults and their man-cubs eat dinner in the back yard like wild animals?

Because it is in the less than idyllic moments that a family is made.

I had to remember this when, weeks after the littles left, another mess settled in our home. This time involving one of our boys.

When new parents bring their bundle of newborn joy home from the hospital, it never occurs to them a day might come when the bundle becomes a handful and you second-guess that trip home from the hospital.

It usually happens sometime between the ages of twelve and twenty. For us, it happened at the ripe old age of sixteen and a half. Three times over. Apparently, at that age, the Cushatt boys' brains begin to pickle and become totally useless.

Not that I'm bitter.

With our second son, it started as a wrestling between childhood and adulthood. Not quite a man, but no longer a little boy. His struggle wasn't entirely unexpected or unusual, more a rite of passage and messy move toward maturity than anything else. The same happened with our oldest and years later with our youngest. But with Ryan, one additional factor wielded far too much influence.

Substance use. The specifics aren't significant, at least not here. It's enough to say this outside force slowly pulled our boy away from us.

The first hint of a struggle showed up on his report card during his sophomore year. He'd always struggled with school, not because he lacked the ability, but because he lacked the motivation. The low grades weren't a red flag in and of themselves. But when they moved from low to borderline failing, in almost every class, our concern grew. Then when he almost didn't make his high school graduation, we knew it was more than a rough phase.

Add to that his change in attitude and change in personality, and we knew something was going on. He wasn't the same easygoing boy, quick to smile and laugh. Instead, he grew agitated and snapped in anger without provocation. Not to mention the constant disagreement, arguing, and lying. Regardless of the subject —values, faith, relationships, education—we stood in polarity. After a lifetime of planting seeds of faith and integrity, we now saw little evidence of either. He seemed bent on becoming the opposite of what we aimed for.

I thought back on Ryan as a little boy, before I felt him start to slip away. He was my quiet, content boy. A calm creek, meandering through life on the path of least resistance. This made him charming, easy to love, and everyone's friend.

But, at times, the very qualities we loved about him also made him more follower than leader. Just as a river is the first to flood in a storm, Ryan was easily carried downstream by youthful impulse and the influence of others. Without the securing banks of discipline and determination, he flowed wherever the weather took him. In high school and the year following, the weather took him farther and farther away from us.

Like many parents, we agonized over this. How did we let this happen? Where did we go wrong? How could we bring him back, save him from himself?

I soon discovered that you can't. Not when he doesn't want to be saved.

One evening in September, only weeks after my last surgery, I heard raised voices upstairs, near the boys' bedrooms. My husband's and my stepson's.

"You need to figure this out, Ryan." Troy's voice carried the exasperation of a father who'd had this same conversation one too many times.

"I'm eighteen years old and it's my life. Stop controlling me and let me live it!" Ryan's voice carried the arrogance of a child who doesn't see his own foolishness and cares little how it impacts others.

"I'm not trying to control you, Ryan. I'm trying to coach you." I could hear the pleading, his desperation to save his son. There's nothing more painful than to feel your child slipping through your fingers.

"You're always telling me what to do. But I'm not you! I don't believe the same things you believe." His anger escalated, his words piercing.

They found their mark. "And how's that working for you? You dropped out of college. You have no money, no plan, no motivation. How long do you think that's going to last?"

Over the next several minutes, barbs flew with deep emotion. I understood our son's desire for independence, remembered feeling the same at eighteen myself. But I also understood my husband's pain, his heart to make one last effort to rescue our child from a danger he couldn't see. In the middle of the volley, something clicked, for both my husband upstairs and me downstairs.

Praying, we came to the same conclusion: we needed to let our son go.

"Ryan, I love you." Troy's voice softened, carrying a seriousness that warned me of what was to come. "Michele and I both love you, more than you know." He paused, probably steeling himself for the hardest words he'd ever have to say.

"Here's the deal. You can't keep living here if you're going to continue making the same choices. You're right. It's your life, and you get to choose. But …"

I knew what was coming, felt the sting of what it would cost us all.

"But this is my house. And if you choose to make choices that we don't agree with, I can't allow you to live here anymore."

We'd talked about this for weeks. Scratch that, months. We knew the stakes, felt tremendous pressure to do the right thing, whatever that was. For a time we thought if we could keep him close, under our roof and eating at our table, we could keep him safe, coach him through this rough patch. But the longer we hung on, the worse it became. Now, with the tension maxed in an upstairs bedroom, we knew the truth: to save the relationship, we had to release it.

Troy continued, said what had to be said even as it broke his heart.

"I have a responsibility to lead this family. And if you won't allow me to help you find a better path, then you need to leave. It's not what we want, but it's your choice."

The next day, our eighteen-year-old son moved out. Choosing a life of pleasure over the parents who loved him.

Weeks later, Troy and I attended the funeral of a nineteen-year-old boy, one of Ryan's friends. We were told alcohol played a role, which wasn't uncommon or surprising with their particular group of friends. But this time the drinking led to a drowning. A split-second decision that ended a life.

It was Troy who delivered the news to Ryan, late on a Friday night, over the phone. I wondered how he would find gentle enough words to tell our son. Death news isn't gentle, no matter how it's delivered. It rips and shreds and changes a life's fabric forever.

We sat in the church, halfway to the back. Two microphones stood like pillars in the front of the auditorium, and friends filed by to share funny stories and fearless adventures. They also talked about the unfairness of death and wept with confusion over the unanswered whys.

It didn't have to be this way!

I wanted to scream those words from my chair, rush to the front to grab Ryan by the shoulders and shake him until he came to his senses. Parents shouldn't have to bury a son. It was an accident. A horrific, terrible, but avoidable accident. I grieved for his mother, felt a physical ache in my chest. As a video displayed pictures of a boy, birth to death, I watched my son and his friends, hoping for some sign of conviction or impact. Instead, I saw only invincible teenagers raging at the unfairness of God but unable to grasp their own culpability.

Then a single thought chilled me: It could be my child in that casket. God forbid, might still be.

For almost half my life, I'd been a mother on a mission: to love my boys and keep them safe.

Look both ways before crossing!

Don't talk to strangers!

Brush your teeth. And don't forget to eat your vegetables!

It wasn't easy teaching these lessons, repeating countless warnings and cautions and keeping them safe from harm. But sitting in the back of a church filled with mourners, I realized that had been the easier part of motherhood. When the greatest dangers included cavities and busy streets, and all a mama needed to do to preserve life was to hold a hand.

The harder part, the part I didn't anticipate when I carried the infant seat out of the maternity ward, is the letting go. When the hands-on season of parenting comes to an end and the out-of-arm's-reach parenting begins. Then, when boys become men and girls become women, parents release their children to write their own stories. And with that, the freedom to experience and endure the outcomes.

It feels like a ripping, this letting go. I liked mothering better when I could manage all the details. Now, with Ryan no longer living in our home, I was forced to watch the movie of my boy's life play out without any means to secure a happy conclusion. Limbo. Horrific, gut-wrenching limbo.

For me, this kind of love required more strength, grace, and forgiveness than I thought I had the capacity to give. Quite honestly, it was one of the hardest things I'd had to do. Like a wounded woman at risk of bleeding out, I wanted to wrap a tourniquet tight and cut off the flow. To shut down, bandage my heart, and protect myself from any further losses. Loving a child who fought against that love hurt too much. And I didn't want to hurt anymore.

When the funeral ended, I found my son in a circle of red-eyed friends. I knew he wanted his friends this day, and I felt far too tentative to arm-wrestle my way into his grief. Instead, I touched him on the shoulder, said his name, and wrapped my arms around my boy.

"I love you. I'm so sorry."

The tension remained high for months following. We continued to communicate, scheduled lunch dates, and shared text messages. But we knew the gap in values remained. No amount of cajoling or convincing changed his mind. Our frustration and helplessness to resolve it exhausted us.

Then, slowly, a stronger, more powerful emotion began to ease the sting of discord.

Love. Unyielding and authentic love.

Not a love based on performance or position, but the kind of love that embraces each other—in-progress child and fallible parent—for who they are today, not who they may or may not become tomorrow.

This is the true test of parenting, when you find your child in a mess of their making and you have to decide whether you'll guard your heart and keep him at arm's length, or love him in the middle of it. Not agree with him, condone his behavior, or rescue him. Maybe not even like him. But there is strength in the person who digs deep to both disagree and love with equal passion. To make convictions known, maybe even say goodbye. But who, at the end of all the tough decisions, has the guts to say, "I love you. And that won't ever change."

This is love in the Land of Limbo. It dives into the mess, no forks or spoons or napkins. It reaches through the wilderness and finds a way to be a family anyway.

A short time later, a tragedy hit our city unexpectedly. A shooting, children and adults alike the unsuspecting victims. I saw it on the news and immediately took account of those I cared about most. My husband sat at the kitchen table. Tyler and Jacob watched television and played video games in bedrooms.

One son wasn't so easily accounted for. Ryan no longer lived a bedroom away, within arm's reach. I couldn't grab his hand or look in his eyes, see him breathing and know he was okay. Feeling that familiar mama-worry, I grabbed my phone and shot him a quick text, hoping he'd answer.

Thinking about you. Want to know if you're okay.

There was more I wanted to—needed to—say. I sent one more message.

I just want you to know that I'm so thankful I got to be your second mom. I love you and am so proud of you.

Hard words to say, considering all the grief and struggle and worry of the months and years before. To say them meant to open myself back up, to risk and love even when I knew it might not be returned. And yet I knew them to be true, even if I didn't have all the answers.

He wrote back, a short time later, with words equally as costly. And equally as true.

I love you too. And thank you for being there.

CHAPTER 15

La Vita è Bella

The real enemies of our life are the "oughts" and the "ifs." They pull us backward into the unalterable past and forward into the unpredictable future. Real life is in the here and now.

—HENRI NOUWEN, *Here and Now*

SHE STOOD A FEW FEET FROM THE HOSPITAL ELEVATOR.

Older than me, maybe late fifties or early sixties, dressed in black slacks, a chic royal blue blouse, and a jewel-toned silk scarf wrapped neatly around her head. I guessed her hair to be silver but didn't see any strands peeking out from beneath the scarf.

Classy, I thought. The epitome of grace, from her choice of fashion to the way she stood, regal, and waited for the elevator doors to open.

It was early November and the day of my semimonthly post-cancer checkup. I heard the ding of the elevator's arrival and climbed inside, along with several others. A stranger stood next to the button panel, finger prepped to push.

"Where's everyone headed?" he asked, waiting.

"Six, please," I answered. The Head and Neck Surgery floor. My home for the twelve months before. A few others called out destinations, including one woman hidden behind all the others in the far corner.

"Twelve," she whispered. I could barely make out her voice, even though she stood only a foot or two away.

The scarf-clad woman smiled in understanding. "I'm headed there too. No one wants to go to the twelfth floor." She chuckled as if sharing some kind of private joke. "But they tell me today might be my last day!" She beamed with her good news.

One or two others laughed along with her, although I doubt they knew why. I certainly didn't. I glanced at the panel holding the key to every floor, hoping to get a clue.

Oncology. The word leapt off the panel next to the number twelve.

I now understood the reason for the woman's soft, pensive voice. The explanation for the other woman's scarf. And the reason she celebrated the prospect of her last visit.

I'd never been to the twelfth floor. One year ago, it had been a strong possibility. As I felt the elevator lift and take us to our different destinations, I was keenly aware of how my story could've turned out differently. By some miracle, I'd been given a best-case scenario. As much as I didn't want another doctor's appointment, I wasn't going to the twelfth floor. Thank God, not the twelfth floor. Too much fear and grief lived there, I knew.

And yet the woman with the scarf didn't stop smiling. In an elevator filled with patients, she exuded the most joy. This both impressed me and convicted me.

A few minutes later, I sat in the now familiar patients' room on the sixth floor. I'd lost track of how many times I'd sat in the same room, on the same examining table. It'd been a little more than eight weeks since my last surgery. I'd recovered, for the most part. The pain lingered, always it lingered, but the cyst hadn't come back yet. Still, Dr. Forrester expected to see me every two months. Especially considering all my complications.

I knew what would happen. She'd evaluate every inch of my mouth and tongue, and palpate all the lymph nodes in my face and neck. She'd done the same countless times before, and I was used to the routine. But this appointment carried more weight than all the others.

A lot of life hinged here. It'd been one year. One year since the phone call and diagnosis rocked my world. Those who have endured a cancer diagnosis know dates function like mile markers in a race. Each one significant, and each one a step closer to the finish. In many ways, it gets harder as you go.

In the span of one year, I'd had three biopsies, several surgeries, and dozens of doctor's appointments. Not to mention the chronic pain. I was over it. I wanted the drama to stop.

But in addition to my own life, the lives of three little children also hinged on this appointment. They'd stayed with us several times over the prior two months, slowly becoming a part of our family. At the time, they remained with a relative, going to school while I healed. But Troy and I had already decided: if Dr. Forrester delivered a "cancer free" pronouncement, the littles were coming home. For good.

In all, the appointment took no more than fifteen minutes. Dr. Forrester poked and prodded, pinched and palpated. Then, removing her headlamp, she settled into her swivel chair.

"You look great." She smiled, knowing the relief I'd feel with those three words. "All's clear. I'll see you in three months. Sound good?"

Cancer free, baby! I had my life back.

If I'd had a bottle of champagne, I would've uncorked it.

Instead, Troy and I spent the drive home discussing our plans to add three children to our family.

We needed to call relatives, rearrange our schedules. Pick up more plastic plates and cups. Buy hairbrushes, barrettes, and extra towels. Troy had spent much of the fall finishing the basement, creating one more bedroom. He was nearly done. Then we'd need to find more beds, twin sheet sets, and pillows and rearrange the furniture. Our family was about to expand, and we had some serious work to do.

Thankfully, we had time to tackle it. It was the beginning of November, and the littles were in the middle of a school year. Only preschool and kindergarten, but we didn't want to disrupt their routine more than necessary. They'd already had enough of that. After talking with their caregiver and working out the details, we wrote the last day of the school semester on the calendar. The countdown had begun.

Aside from all the shopping and rearranging, a big part of our preparation involved getting our marriage ready for another round of parenting. In the spring, we'd celebrated our tenth anniversary. Sort of. Cancer, rude character that it is, stole the show. We didn't get to celebrate as planned.

Years before, we'd dreamed of an epic trip to celebrate our ten-year anniversary: a trip to Italy. We saved for it well ahead of time, fifty dollars here, one hundred there. I took on extra writing projects and speaking engagements just to fill the Italy fund. It'd been our dangling carrot, the additional motivation to hang on to each other and keep moving forward. Surviving a remarriage and blended family for a decade deserved an award.

But then cancer showed up, curse it. And three children needing a home, bless them. And our Italy tickets for two had to be postponed indefinitely.

Until November, when the doctor said "cancer free." And we realized we had a window of exactly four weeks before life changed.

It's now or never, I remember thinking.

Cancer taught us this, that waiting for later can be a pricey gamble. The unexpected happens, contrary to our best laid plans, and later may never come. But today we had life, each other, and a marriage worth fighting for. Three littles needed a home and a family, including two parents more in love than they were on the day of their wedding.

That's why on November 11, Troy and I boarded a United Airlines airplane with hearts full of hope and stupid silly grins.

A middle-of-the-marriage honeymoon. Cancer free, crazy in love, and Italy bound.

~

I didn't expect the emotion.

Thrill and exhilaration, yes. Tears, no.

We'd arrived in Rome little more than an hour before. After dropping our bags, we left our hotel room to explore the sights and sounds of the ancient city.

Rome! We're in Rome!

Within a short walk, we crossed over from storefronts with modern fashion displays to stone walkways lined with aged crumbling walls. My fingers brushed centuries-old stones as we walked down the streets of ancient Rome. The sun had set a half hour before, allowing stars older than the stones to illuminate the streets.

Cars honked and jockeyed for position on the crowded streets. Traffic lights glittered red and green. Policemen whistled and directed pedestrians and traffic. But the contemporary sights and sounds hardly registered. I'd traveled back in time.

Whether it was the darkness, the Rome-ness, or simply my awe at the wealth of history within arm's reach, I couldn't speak. Emotion welled up from a deep and sacred space as my fingers touched the stones that had survived to tell their stories. The lump in my throat surprised me, but perhaps it shouldn't have.

This was *my* history. Maybe not directly, like the passing of bloodlines and brown eyes. But in a way that felt far more significant.

A piece of my faith had its roots here. And for as long as I could remember, faith had been my anchor. I loved history, biblical history in particular. To me, the Bible's characters—Moses, Paul, and so many others—weren't fictional characters spun of a writer's imagination. They were real, flesh-and-blood people who married, birthed children, celebrated holidays, and worked honest jobs. From the moment I learned to read, I studied their stories, pictured their faces, and imagined their emotions. Now, years later, they felt as much a part of my family as my own aunts, uncles, and grandparents. In many ways, more so.

I looked at the stones under my feet, reached my hand to feel the cold, smooth surface of another bit of a wall. I could feel the nearness of others, their breaths on my neck. Paul had been here. Early Jesus-followers had thrived and suffered here. They lived and died with the hope of eternity on their lips.

What courage! Two thousand years before, ordinary men and women, not all that different from me, chose death over disbelief because of their confidence in something greater, someone bigger. Two millennia had passed, millions of lives come and gone. I thought of myself, my short forty years of life on this earth. I thought of my struggle over the months before and how I'd let cancer and my fear of death nearly consume my life. I too chose death. But a living death because of my unbelief.

I stopped walking to look up at an ancient wall butting up to a modern one. The contrast powerful, the implications unmistakable. Two worlds colliding in the space of a few feet. Old and new. Then and now.

How foolish I'd been! On the streets of Rome on a cool November night, I linked hands with Troy, mingling my fingers with his. With my husband on one side and history on the other, I heard the stones speak of the power of faith. Of believing what you cannot see, of banking a life on something more real and powerful than the certainty of death.

No one spoke, but something changed.

Faith. *I choose faith!* Emboldened by the courage of so many brave others who'd gone before, I determined to live a different life. I didn't know what that looked like exactly. But I knew I didn't want a legacy characterized by regret over the past and fear of the future. I wanted the stones of my life to speak of a deep and enduring faith. Regardless of the cost.

~

"You sit and read. I'll go grab a few things," he said with feigned nonchalance. It was our last night in Italy, and I knew he planned to make it memorable.

Normally, I wouldn't let him do all the work while I lounged with a book. But the look on his face convinced me he needed to do this. And I needed to let him. It didn't take all that much convincing.

"Alright. Meet back here in a half hour?"

By "back here" I meant the Spanish Steps, the Piazza di

Spagna. A popular tourist spot, rich with stories and history, it sat only a couple of blocks from our hotel room. I could read a book by the fountain, and people-watch. The day was brisk but sunny, and I had all the time in the world. Why not?

Troy disappeared into the crowd. I settled next to the fountain and opened my Kindle.

I'd been told that in 1821 and at the age of twenty-five, poet John Keats died in an apartment on the right corner of the piazza. Other artists and writers claimed this spot for their inspiration. As I watched tourists and locals pass through the piazza, I imagined that the scene didn't look all that different when Keats paused in his writing to look out his window and take in the crowds. Time had passed, but much of life had stayed the same. Another hundred years from now, I'd be the memory, and new tourists would fill the piazza wondering about those who sat at the same fountain years before.

Close to an hour passed before Troy returned. He sneaked up behind me, a bulging package underneath his arm.

"What've you got there?"

"You'll see," he winked. "Let's walk."

The sun was just beginning to lower over the western sky. We climbed the Spanish Steps—one hundred and thirty-five of them—to get the best view of the city.

We turned after the last stair to take in the view of Rome. Exquisite. Beyond words. As the sun lowered, Troy pulled out our SLR camera and snapped several shots. Soft pinks and browns softened the scene, and Rome expanded impossibly wide in front of us. We could see St. Peter's Basilica standing proud and magnificent in the distance, the cupola golden in the waning light. Straight ahead, over miles of stone-paved streets, the Colosseum and the Forum prepared to close for the evening. Piazzas, fountains, and cathedrals dotted the cityscape, such that you couldn't walk a half dozen blocks without stumbling into another rich piece of history.

Standing at the top of the Spanish Steps, we saw the prior eleven days we'd spent together in Italy. Intimate, sacred days that would anchor our marriage for the life awaiting us back at home.

Troy reached for my hand. "Let's go."

I hated to leave the view at the top of the steps, but there was more to see. We turned left and walked up the street, taking us farther away from our hotel and the familiar. In all our exploring of Rome, we'd never made it to this section. Everything was new and fresh to us, and I couldn't help but wish we had another day or two. No matter how much time you have, it's never quite enough.

"We have to come back, you know." My words sounded more like a question than a statement.

Even after eleven days of soaking up everything Italy had to offer, I wanted more. I needed to know we'd do things like this again, husband-and-wife things, even after our lives and schedules grew by three more children. I wanted my husband to promise me that.

"Absolutely," he reassured.

I believed him, but I wondered how tough it would be to make good on that promise. It's one thing to say it, another to make it happen while parenting six kids.

Ahead, we saw the entrance to the Villa Borghese garden. This was where we were headed, to find a quiet park bench that overlooked the city while the sun set in the distance.

As crowded as the Piazza di Spagna, the garden of Villa Borghese remained quiet. A few couples strolled hand in hand. Pet owners walked their dogs. Children laughed and played on a small merry-go-round in the center of the park.

We moved away from the children and dog-walkers on instinct, wanting to savor these last precious moments, just the two of us. We'd have plenty of children sounds once we got home. For now, we needed each other.

The path wound through a canopy of trees, the dark-green leaves shading the dwindling twilight. Four-foot pillars held the granite busts of famous Italians and lined the walkway. We found an empty park bench placed underneath one of these stone faces. Other than him, we were alone.

The bench sat away from the main path and provided a partial view of the city. Spectacular. All of it. The buildings. The people. The food and wine and conversation. The way the city seemed to come alive each day as the sun set. Even Italy's cappuccino, served in itty-bitty cups, made the perfect complement to the pastries we couldn't get enough of. The entire trip had been the makings of a fairytale, a dream come true.

I settled into the bench, wrapped my sweater around my shoulders.

"You hungry?" Troy opened his bag, revealing the contents. A thick bunch of red grapes. A loaf of crusty bread. Slices of salami and fresh mozzarella. A full bottle of Merlot. And two plastic cups.

"I don't have wine glasses. Sorry."

"Who needs wine glasses?" I had everything I could ever want, right here, with him. "This is perfect. Every bit of it."

For an hour, give or take, we snuggled on a park bench in the middle of a Roman garden. We ate our simple feast and watched the sun lower and fade. As the light dimmed, I leaned into our final dwindling moments in Rome as husband and wife.

"I love you. You know that, right?" I looked at him over my wine, met his eyes in the soft light.

He smiled, his eyes wrinkling at the corners and twinkling in that way that always melts me. "I do. And I love you."

Cancer, as heinous and evil as it was, had delivered an unexpected gift.

It taught us how to live. Not in regret over all the ways we wished we could go back and do it over. Not in mourning the countless unfinished, undone places that yet remained. And not in fear of the unknown future we couldn't predict or control.

Cancer—in both its presence and absence—had taught me the immeasurable value of *today*. Faith isn't rooted in the past or the future. It's birthed in how we approach and handle today. It's the anchor that holds us firmly in this moment, allowing us the freedom to experience it and enjoy it regardless of the regrets and what-ifs. Those who have faith, deep abiding faith in an Artist who has all things under his control, have no need to rehash the past or predict the future. They're content to sit on a park bench, sip wine, and watch the sunset with the one they love.

"Now faith is confidence in what we hope for and assurance about what we do not see. This is what the ancients were commended for."[20]

This is the story of which the stones whispered when we first arrived in Rome. And the reason the beautiful scarved-woman could smile in spite of her trip to the twelfth floor.

Because we know what's coming. That means that for today, for this moment, *la vita è bella*.

Life is beautiful.

CHAPTER 16

No Room

Reader, what have you done since this church opened to make it a benefit to mankind? We trust your entire duty to this mission. This church extended a helping hand to the poor people outside of this church. Do you allow the poor to enter this church with the same welcome as those in costly robes?

—AUTHOR UNKNOWN, January 20, 1889
(penciled on a rafter in the attic of Trinity United Methodist Church, Denver, CO)

PREPARATIONS FOR A GUEST ARE FAR DIFFERENT THAN FOR A resident.

I learned this at the end of November, after Troy and I returned from Italy. We'd had plenty of visitors in our years of marriage. Some stayed for a week or a weekend. Others moved in for a month or two during a time of transition. To prepare, I stocked up on extra groceries, changed the sheets on the guest bed, and set out clean towels. For some, we rearranged schedules and canceled appointments. But always a day came, regardless of the length of stay, when the guest packed up and headed home. Afterward life returned to normal, the way it'd been before the visitor arrived.

Not so with a resident. When someone moves in, he becomes a fellow dweller and part of the family. Whether a new spouse or an aging in-law—or, let's say, three preschoolers—everything changes. Not for a week or two. For as long as they remain.

Furniture. Budget. Grocery list. Kitchen sink. Vehicle. Family vacations. Routines. Bedtimes. Expectations. Date night. Laundry pile. Free time. Extended family. Friendships.

Visitors can be accommodated. Residents must be assimilated.

The night before the littles moved into our home, the truth of what we were about to do hit me like a speeding train. I sat on the mocha Berber carpet in my fourteen-year-old's bedroom—*former* bedroom—as he and Troy assembled a borrowed set of bunk beds. It didn't look like my boy's room anymore. Gone was the student desk and the posters pinned to his wall. He'd moved all his clothes and furniture out earlier in the day, taking over the bedroom in the basement. Far away from his room across the hall from mine.

By this time tomorrow, we'll have three more children. Four- and five-year-olds. In our house.

For months we'd been hoping for this moment, praying and planning for it. I thought I wanted it. Now, with reality staring back at me in the form of two bunk beds, I wasn't so sure.

Maybe my hesitation was a result of our nearly twenty years of experience. We didn't harbor the dreamy illusions of first-time parents who can't wait to bring their baby home. We knew the flip side of all that preciousness, how little true parenting resembles a Hallmark commercial. The sleeplessness, bathroom accidents, and never-ending worry. The drama, throw-ups, and late nights of homework. And the constant need for a parent to be on her game, ready to love and sacrifice and pour herself out for the sake of the bundle she brought home from the hospital.

Or maybe my apprehension prickled as a result of our current scenario. We were neck deep in parenting adolescents. Ours were good boys. Still, even good boys struggle their way into manhood. This wasn't exactly the vacation part of the parenting trip. Tension continued to rattle our house on a daily basis, and we couldn't box up that part of our life and put it to the side. Three new children didn't replace the existing ones.

Troy and Jacob worked together to screw the headboard and baseboard and join the end posts together, lifting the second bed on top of the first, attaching the ladder and side rails and setting both mattresses in place.

I stood back, holding two sets of twin-size sheets. Mute and wide-eyed.

"You okay?" Troy must've seen my pasty-white cheeks, locked knees, or some other indication that I was about to keel over in a faint.

I swallowed, tried to hide my uncertainty. "This is really happening."

"Yes. True." Holding his blue Makita screwdriver in one hand, he stopped working long enough to measure me with his eyes. "You haven't changed your mind, have you? You still want to do this?"

I did. Of course I did.

Except, I didn't.

Two powerful and conflicting emotions trying to set up house in my stomach.

Troy is notorious for seeing life in black and white, while I tend to view it in hues of gray. How did I explain my ambiguity to the man who'd just barn-raised two bunk beds? He worked with certainty. How did I confess the strange grief I was beginning to feel? That I both mourned and celebrated the adventure yet to come?

"Yes. Of course I do." It was the right answer, the expected answer. I rolled my shoulders, trying to rid my back of tension. "It's hard to take in, that's all."

He turned his attention back to the bed, leaving me to my thoughts. But I didn't want the conversation to end. I had more to get off my chest.

"Our lives will never be the same. You know that, right?" I hoped he might share my conflicting emotions.

He held the screwdriver to the post of a bed corner and glanced over his shoulder at me. "Yep. I know." He turned back to the post and drove the screw into the hole. "That's kind of the point, isn't it?"

He was right. Matter-of-fact and not exactly tender, but right. We'd prayed about this. Spent countless nights talking about it. From the first phone call, we could see evidence of divine orchestration. The intricate weaving and aligning of desire and circumstance to bring this family together.

I just hadn't expected my easy prayers to solicit such uncomfortable answers.

Less than twenty-four hours later, after the beds were ready and the refrigerator full, three children burst through our garage door and infiltrated the house. Shrieks and squeals echoed off the hardwood floors. The children bounced and pounced and chattered more than a Tigger playing with Pooh. Happy. Crazy, over-the-top happy. Like children who'd waited a lifetime to come home.

"I put my bag in my bed-woom." Jack skipped through the foyer and climbed the stairs, his hand cupping the wood rail all the way to the top. He knew exactly where to go, what to do.

Princess and Peanut followed close on his heels, running into their neighboring room and flopping on their beds.

"Bunk beds!" They cheered, at least two octaves higher than anything our home had heard before. The previous night's efforts did not go unnoticed.

In minutes, the once-clean family room filled with toys, coloring books, and winter coats and shoes thrown off in enthusiasm. The bedrooms, the very same bedrooms my boys had occupied only the day before, were now littered with stuffed animals, baby blankets, and rows of Dr. Suess and children's Bibles.

The air left my lungs.

My too-big house suddenly felt far too small.

God, forgive me. I hid in a corner of my bedroom and cried.

~

The first weeks of any major change are often the hardest. Such was the case with us, although our transition wouldn't end after a handful of weeks. It would take months and years for us to recapture any sense of normalcy. The English language does not contain adequate words to describe the proportions of our familial transition.

Monumental? Colossal? Mammoth? Not even close.

Naturally, as I typically do when feeling all measure of pain and discomfort, I resorted to questioning our decision. How did this happen? What had I been thinking? Better yet, what was *Troy* thinking? He's supposed to be the stable one.

As my gut predicted on the night of the bunk beds, everything changed. Even before the children arrived, ours was a full life, with three kids, two careers, and a marriage. Then, like an already full river trying to absorb the rain from a downpour, our family went from capacity to overflowing. We all felt like we were drowning.

Then the arrival of Christmas. The unexpected respite in my rain.

We have few nonnegotiable traditions in our family, but Christmas Eve delivers two of them. After a dinner of potato-cheese soup and homemade bread (not a nonnegotiable, but a tradition nonetheless), we drive downtown. There, dwarfed by Denver's skyline and warmed by her Christmas lights, we make two stops. First, the Denver Rescue Mission. Second, Trinity United Methodist Church.

Christmas Eve we did just as we always had, but with a bigger crew. Earlier that evening, after dinner, I drew three baths, washed three heads of hair, and toweled each of my littles dry. Searching a closet filled with hand-me-downs from friends and family, I found two dresses of black velvet and red taffeta, sizes four and five. For Jack, I pulled out a bright red sweater and khaki dress pants, miniatures of the same hanging in Troy's closet. I slipped silky dresses over wet heads, pulled pants up, and helped tie shoes. Then, awkwardly since I didn't yet know how to fix girl hair, I brushed and blow-dried until all three heads shone like the lights on our tree.

This was my new life. Already the old life, the life before, began to fade.

Just as we'd done three hundred and sixty-five days before, we loaded up and drove toward downtown Denver. Only this time we needed two cars to get us all there. Two adults, six children, and Tyler's girlfriend, Cassie. The nine members of the Cushatt family.

First, the Denver Rescue Mission. Our stop lasted less than fifteen minutes, long enough to transfer boxes of food and clothes and toys from car trunks to mission kitchen. It had looked like so much when I bought it at the store and packed it into our car. But

I knew it wouldn't be enough to serve the hundreds of homeless who would file through on a single day. Too small. Our offering was far too small.

Back in the car, I glanced in the rearview mirror to gauge the faces of the littles. Light from the mission's "Jesus Saves" sign filtered through the windows to reflect in their eyes. Three homeless men loitered on the sidewalk not twenty feet from where our car idled at the curb. They took it all in—the light, the old brick building, the grimy, lost-looking men.

"This is the Denver Rescue Mission," I tried to explain. "Homeless people—people who don't have a house like we do—come here. The mission gives them food and a bed for the night." I waited to see if they understood. "Did you know that some people don't have food or a home?"

They stared back at me in the mirror, the quietest they'd been in days. Of course they knew.

By the time we arrived at Trinity, the candlelight service was about to start. Late had become the new normal for us. In spite of our best efforts, we just couldn't seem to get everyone where they needed to be on time. We searched for a place to sit, but churchgoers filled every wooden pew. I could see seats for one or two here and there, but not enough for nine. I wouldn't split us up. No way. More than ever before, we needed to be a family, sit together. But where? There was no place for a family our size to go.

A woman, older, decked out in her best holiday dress, motioned to us. We followed her, hoping she knew of an empty pew we hadn't been able to find. She turned left, taking us down a side hallway. Maybe to the staircase and balcony?

She passed the stairs, made another turn, our family following like obedient little chicks connected in one long chain of hands. About the time I'd lost all direction and wondered if we'd ever find our way out, she opened a thick wooden door and pointed to a long row of empty chairs.

More than enough for all nine of us to sit together.

In the choir loft. On the stage. In front of the entire room of gaping parishioners.

You've got to be kidding me.

I turned, certain we'd fallen for some kind of joke. But she was gone.

This would not end well.

While it's true my preschool parenting skills had grown a bit rusty, I remembered enough to know you don't prop three small children and three adolescent boys on a platform an hour before midnight. Not on the most sacred night of Christendom's calendar year. And not without calling in the national guard and throwing me a stash of fruit snacks.

What should we do? Sit and risk turning Christmas Eve into a circus for a roomful of worshipers? Or split our family on a night that was far more sacred to us than anyone could know?

The nine Cushatts filed in and sat down. On the stage.

Have mercy.

In a move of strategic parental brilliance, Troy and I alternated big kids with small kids, placing our moderately mature selves at equal intervals in between. And we started praying. And fasting. And calling on the angelic hosts of heaven.

Choir members, sitting down front in their perfectly pressed white robes, turned to take in the family of nine sitting behind. I could see their confusion. Or was it panic? I feigned nonchalance, as if putting a family onstage for the length of a church service was an everyday occurrence. I turned to the audience, noticed the hundreds of round eyes staring back at me. I'm pretty sure they thought we were part of the show.

Dear God, I hope not.

Although I expected our kindly usher to return with additional latecomers, she never reappeared. That Christmas Eve night, the Cushatt family alone populated the church platform. Behind the robed choir and the line of reverend church staff, we celebrated the birth of Jesus from the best seats in the house.

Two thousand years ago when a young man and pregnant woman traveled by road and donkey to a Bethlehem inn, they didn't receive the same welcome.

"While they were there, the time came for the baby to be born, and she gave birth to her firstborn, a son. She wrapped him in cloths and placed him in a manger, because there was no guest room available for them."[21]

We know little about that Christmas Eve night. Two parents showed up in Bethlehem, the mother swollen with child. They searched for a place to rest, where they could be together. But the innkeeper couldn't spare a single room. His home was too full to add three more.

I wonder, at times, if the innkeeper's refusal was more personal than logistical. Surely he'd had a corner where an expectant mother could've slept. And what about his room? Couldn't he have sacrificed his own bed for a single night? Maybe his lacking wasn't in home but in heart.

Sitting center-stage with a four-year-old leaning on my arm, I saw myself in Bethlehem's innkeeper. In spite of my proclamations of love and service, I'd grown to love comfort more. It'd become my addiction, my idol. I didn't know this, at least not fully, until discomfort interrupted my comfortable life in the shape and form of three little people at my front door. I wanted a life of convenience. Saturday morning sleep-ins, a clean kitchen, vacuumed floors. The freedom to go where I wanted, when I wanted, without burden or surrender.

I still wanted to think myself generous. At times I was. Didn't I box up food for the homeless? Didn't I make meals for the sick? Yes, and yes. But rarely did my offerings stretch me to a place of inconvenience and discomfort. Of sacrifice.

The reverend took his place behind the podium. With Bible spread wide, he told the story of Mary, Joseph, and a child whose ordinary manger birth rocked a hope-hungry world.

God dressed in flesh. Leaving the comfort and glory of heaven, he took on pain, illness, emotion, and heartache. He chose to exchange his world for ours, his bedroom for a stable. So that, someday, when we show up at heaven's door, we won't hear the words, "No room!"

My little girl's head slipped into my lap, tired beyond her years and rocked to sleep by the preacher's voice and the choir's songs. I circled one arm around her shoulders, pulled the fingers of my hand through her hair.

So this is what it's like to have a little girl, I thought. *This is what it feels like to be a mama all over again.*

His story and message done, the reverend found his chair as the choir began to sing, a cappella.

Silent night, holy night.
All is calm, all is bright.

The ushers walked through the darkened room, lighting candles. Soon light spread, filling the room with illuminated faces. I looked down my row, seeing the smiles of those I loved most in the world. Each one different from the others. Some delivered through birth. Others through marriage and unexpected circumstances. Each a gift, regardless of how they came.

Twelve months before, I'd hovered on the brink of life and death. I'd never imagined that, one year later, God would bring me to my own Bethlehem to give birth to a new family.

Round yon virgin, mother and child.
Holy infant, so tender and mild.

I looked down at the girl in my lap, a girl I hardly knew, and watched her chest rise and fall, her eyes flutter in dreamy sleep. Like the subtle brush of angel wings, I felt the first stirrings of a mother's love. A child is born!

God help me, I didn't want mine to be the innkeeper's story. I could cry, "No room!" and get a good night's sleep. But then I'd miss seeing the Christ.

A couple of weeks later, I'd tell a trusted friend, Melissa, about Christmas Eve, how a late-night candlelight service and nine chairs on a stage helped me see the truth of our scenario.

"Just because something is hard doesn't mean we're not called to it," I'd tell her. "And just because it's hard doesn't mean it's not good."

Yes. And yes.

God left the comfort of heaven for a complicated, uncomfortable human life. The world has never seen a calling more difficult. Nor a calling more good.

The sacrifice required to redeem a life.

The light offered in the darkness.

With that I offered my bed for three children. And to the sound of "Silent Night" I made room for whatever would come.

Sleep in heavenly peace,
sleep in heavenly peace.[22]

CHAPTER 17

Attached

To love is to assume an infinite debt.

—SØREN KIERKEGAARD,
"Our Duty to Remain in Love's
Debt to One Another"

"You're a bad mommy!"

His words couldn't have hurt me more if he'd grabbed a knife and run me through.

"I don't wike this family! I want to live wif someone else!" He threw his weight against my favorite living room chair, an effort to overturn it in angry punctuation. He aimed to cause me pain. It was working.

"Jack, sweetheart, you need to calm down. Look at me for a minute." After several weeks of living together in the same house, I knew if I could get his eyes to connect with mine, maybe he'd settle, feel safe. Instead, he avoided eye contact. He looked everywhere except at me, a cornered animal looking to flee.

"No!"

The windows rattled with his screams as he ran away from me. My head pounded, hands shook. I looked at this boy, not yet old enough to read. So tiny, and yet so angry. I didn't recognize him.

He turned and glared from beneath furrowed brows, his cheeks flushed with fury, hands balled into fists. This wasn't a mood swing or bad moment. This was his pattern, almost every day.

I cringed at what the neighbors must think, certain they heard his rampage through walls and windows. My boy appeared entirely charming when playing in the front yard. No trace of an alter ego during those brief public appearances. But inside, this. What horrors did they imagine happened in our house, something awful enough to cause a preschooler to scream?

If only they knew. This time, I'd asked him to put his socks away.

The ridiculousness of his anger triggered my own. I could feel the pressure mounting in my shoulders and back, my cheeks turning hot. It wasn't fair the way he commandeered our family with his unpredictable and irrational rage. I'd given up everything for him! And what for? To watch this monster overrun my family.

Still. I reminded myself of his story, of the deep pain that triggered his Hulk-like transformation. Behind the tantrum huddled a little boy trapped by profound fear and anguish.

It's not his fault. It's not his fault. It's not his fault.

Like the boy in Hollywood's movie *Hook*, my Jack felt the losses of too many broken promises. Too young to understand the whys and hows of his losses, he only knew he felt a deep and unyielding pain.

He stormed upstairs, spreading his fury to every corner of the house. Troy waited in the kitchen, giving me space to work an intervention, knowing a two-against-one approach would only make things worse. The girls, anxious to escape the sounds of conflict, rushed out the back door to bubble themselves with play. My older boys hid in their rooms. No one wanted to deal with yet another meltdown.

I climbed the stairs, took a breath, and tried to steady my shaking hands.

I found him in his room. "You're okay, buddy. I'm here." I reached for him, to pull him close. "I'm not going anywhere. I love you." Seldom did this work; I knew this. I tried anyway. Maybe I could love him to wholeness.

Instead.

"I don't love you!" He pulled away from me, hard. Threw his pillows and toys on the floor. Kicked a bedroom door and moved to do the same to our beloved dog, Nika. She hid behind my legs, trying to find safety.

That did it. This time he'd gone too far.

"Stop it!"

My heart pounded a percussion in my chest. Only a thin thread of control kept me from unleashing on this forty-pound child I no longer recognized.

God, help me!

"You need to stop. *Now.*" I tried to bring my voice down but wasn't having much luck. I wanted to scream. "I don't care how angry you are, you aren't allowed to hurt people. Or dogs. Period."

Surprised by my outburst, he hesitated for a moment. This was my chance. I picked him up, his size no match for my own. Sat us both down on his bed.

The feel of him in my arms softened me, just enough.

"I love you, Jack."

My touch did not have the same effect on him. Defiant, he struggled against me, thrashed like a child possessed.

"You're hurting me! You're hurting me!" Of course, I wasn't hurting him. I was holding him, hugging him, rocking him like the baby I imagined him to be before that day we met in a Walmart parking lot.

"I love you. I love you." Back and forth I rocked, repeating the words, murmuring in the soft voice of a mother soothing her newborn son.

In response, he grabbed my arm, dug fingernails in flesh until I could feel my skin give way. Then he moved to my neck, scratching deep lines in the soft tissue.

For once, compassion trumped my anger. A miracle, a pouring out of mercy for both him and me. As he screamed, I prayed.

God, help! I don't know what to do!

I pulled his hands away and kept rocking, offering "I love you's" like gifts, swallowing my anger and pain in an attempt to soothe his.

Then, just as fast as his tempest began, he calmed. Out of control one moment, calm the next. An entirely different child, my little boy started to cry.

"I want Biscuit," he whimpered, asking for his favorite stuffed animal.

I found the treasured toy in a corner of his bed and handed it to him. "Here you go, buddy. Biscuit."

Pulling his puppy close, he nestled his head in between my shoulder and chin, melted against me. No longer pushing me away. No longer running and fighting. Again I started to rock. Back and forth, back and forth.

He'd come back. My boy had come back to me. Wherever he went during those moments of screaming and ranting, he'd returned. I could see it in his eyes, the way he now looked into mine, appearing so very lost and small and unsure.

"I love you, Jack. You know that, don't you?" I brushed his hair with my hand, his head hot and damp.

He nodded, sniffled. I could feel the warmth of his breath on my chest, his heart pounding as fast as mine.

"How much do I love you?"

"A wot." He answered without hesitation, a boy who'd heard the question enough times in the past weeks to know the answer.

"And will I ever stop?"

"No." He nestled deeper underneath my chin, his arms and Biscuit tucked between the warmth of our bodies. Back and forth, back and forth.

In all, his rage lasted about an hour. Not a record, but intense. A few minutes later, he'd put away the socks that had triggered his outburst, a task that would've taken him seconds but instead cost us far more.

For the rest of the day, we limped along like an ordinary family, pretended we didn't have monsters lurking in our closets. But underneath our charade, I agonized over a truth I could no longer ignore.

What if he wasn't fixable? What if the love of our family wasn't enough to heal his wounds and undo the damage that had already been done? What would we do then?

I didn't know. I just didn't know.

~

When we brought our children home, we had no clue about the baggage that came home along with their single suitcase.

Our nearly two decades of parenting had fooled us into believing we were prepared for this new adventure. We knew how to teach little ones to read, say please and thank you, and use forks and napkins (albeit marginally). We could run carpool, help with homework, and say bedtime prayers. We'd even endured the tumultuous teen years, with crises far more complicated than manners and prayers. But we did it, made it to the other side. Mostly unscathed.

Three more children? We could totally do this. High fives all around.

Or not.

Parenting the second time would have little in common with the first. There's a difference between the children born to stable, functioning adults and those who, instead, find their entrance into the world to be far less welcoming.

Six weeks ago, a friend of mine had a baby. Recently, we were at the same conference, and during a break I asked to hold her little one.

"I need a baby fix." I opened my arms and batted my best puppy dog eyes. As much as I didn't want to return to diapers and bottles, I also missed it something fierce.

And so, standing in an ordinary hotel hallway, I held ten pounds of new life. Even after mothering six children, I've yet to get over the miracle of it. Her downy head nuzzled in the elbow of my left arm while my right arm cradled her length. I wrapped myself around her, and although time had slipped me into new seasons of parenting, my body moved just as it'd done years before. Leaning from one leg to the other, I swayed back and forth, back and forth.

The rocking brought revelation: this is what my Jack had missed.

Something so simple, the cradling of a child in a mama's arms. This is what every newborn needs, as much as milk and sleep and dry diapers. Security and warmth. A belonging place.

As I held my friend's newborn, I remembered holding my own. When Jacob, my biological son, was born, I spent countless hours losing myself in those beautiful round eyes so like mine.

I talked in a special voice saved only for him, made faces and shared secrets and worked oh-so-hard to solicit the smallest grin or giggle. Time stood still. To-do lists and schedules disappeared. He was all that mattered.

As a new mother, I'd rocked and talked baby-speak without understanding the long-term implications. I did it because that's what you do when your baby cries or wakes up from a nap or needs dinner. You touch and hold, comfort and nourish, whisper and sing. Even when you're tired. Even when you'd rather hang out with friends or collapse on the couch and watch TV.

I'd had no idea how important my touch was to the children and adults my littles would one day become. Now, as mama to three littles who carry a suitcase packed with fear and anxiety everywhere they go, I know better.

Moments between mother and child aren't ordinary. They're sacred.

What happens between mother and child, father and child, gives an infant, a child, a sense of who they are in connection to someone else. Although individual and unique, a child can grow into that individuality only through the security of connection. Psychologists call it "attachment," the necessary bonding of individuals in relationship to others. It is in relationship with significant others that a child gains a sense of who he is apart.

Without attachment, a child flounders. Like a boat without a sea, a bird without a sky, unattached children feel uncomfortable in their own skin. As a buoy bobs according to the weather and waves, an unattached child vacillates from calm to chaos in the span of seconds. The slightest provocation can unmoor. I'd seen it again and again.

The way Jack unraveled at a change in routine or schedule.

His inability to do simple tasks—the folding of socks or picking up of toys—without a meltdown.

The way he screamed in terror at ordinary houseflies.

Not to mention Peanut's penchant for taking toys and trinkets from friends at school, without thought or remorse. And Princess's crazy lying and elaborate fabrications, delivered with expert skill and manipulation.

When a child can't trust the presence and protection of a parent, they learn the only person they can count on is self. So they do what's necessary to survive. Lie. Steal. Manipulate. Hoard. Rage. And always, always maintain absolute control.

~

He left it in the middle of my desk on his way out the door for another day of school. A sixteen-by-twenty poster with the four letters of his name spelled out in fat black-and-red marker.

J-A-C-K.

I knew why he put it there, in the middle of my office, the center of my desk. Because he knew that's where I'd sit working while he went to school. He didn't want to take a chance I'd forget about him.

As if I could forget.

Soon after his arrival, Troy and I nicknamed him Radar. Both an affectionate and accurate name. Because from the moment he woke in the morning until he went to bed at night, he pinged the world with constant reminders of his existence.

Incessant chatter. Nonsense questions. Crying, whining, and every other manner of making himself known. And a steady and unending bombardment of "I love you's."

I'd come in from the garage: "I love you, Mommy." I'd

pass through the family room where he played with his sisters: "Mommy, I love you." I headed upstairs to go to the bathroom: "Mommy? I love you." Over and over, he pinged me with those four words, words that grated more than warmed by the hundredth hearing.

His "I love you's" weren't so much a declaration of feeling as a compulsive exposure of need. Somewhere along the way he learned that the only way to hear those words is to say them first. Behind each offering lurked desperate, gaping questions:

Do you see me?

Do you like me?

Am I good enough?

I knew this. So I offered one hundred "I love you's" in return, hoping my words would meet his need, fill his gaping hole.

Only they didn't. Minutes later, he'd find me hidden in my office or bathroom and ping me once more. Or he'd leave a sixteen-by-twenty poster in the center of my desk with the four letters of his name in black-and-red marker.

Bless his heart. I could poke my own eyes out.

His never-assuaged neediness frustrated the life out of me. Not the clingy type, I'd never been the mom who needed my children to need me desperately. Instead, I fostered independence, self-sufficiency. To have a child so codependent stretched thin my last nerve.

Intellectually, I understood the why behind his behavior. My heart hurt for him. So I kept pouring, pouring, pouring myself into his cavernous black hole, hoping my offerings would bring some measure of filling. I determined to fix him, bandage his wounds and turn him into a "normal" boy with the magic of my supermama love.

Instead, like a bucket without a bottom, all the love and kindnesses I poured spilled out his holes.

How long could I keep this up? It didn't make sense to keep giving to someone who couldn't receive it. Who pours money into a bad investment? Why spend myself for someone who has no appreciation of the cost?

Isn't that what I did? With the cross?

Holy two-by-four. God whacked me upside the head.

The cross. The single most significant and foolhardy investment of all time. A sacrificial offering, made once for all, for a people who'd never appreciate the cost. People who would scoff at it only moments after receipt.

And what for? To help an unmoored people know they had a place to anchor.

Jack and I are no different. I may be older, taller, and dressed in grown-up clothes. I may have a good job, a solid circle of family and friends, even a few talents that give me a sense of place and purpose. But all it takes is a bad day or bad moment to cause me to spiral into a gaping black hole of insecurity.

It's hard to admit this, to shine light behind my well-polished, together exterior, to expose the girl who wants to be loved but secretly fears she's not worth it. I'd like to think I've grown beyond that, don't need the love I clearly crave. But the evidence is too obvious.

A friend sends a hurtful email. A reader leaves a disparaging comment. A group of friends doesn't include me in an outing. I may not rage, but I can transform from happy to despairing in record time. Then, like Jack, I ping the world with reminders that I exist. A dozen social-media posts and hours spent measuring the replies. Text messages to a handful of friends, hoping to hear a kind word back.

I chase people and position, hoping for enough affirmation to make me feel better about myself. I call, write, schedule my days until each moment explodes with the noise of my life. Behind all this activity, all these pings, sits a single need: to know my existence in this world matters.

The science of it is plain. John Cacioppo and William Patrick, in their book *Loneliness: Human Nature and the Need for Social Connection*, explain it this way: "If you asked a zookeeper to create a proper enclosure for the species Homo sapiens, she would list at the top of her concerns 'obligatorily gregarious,' meaning that you do not house a member of the human family in isolation, any more than you house a member of [Emperor penguins] in hot desert sand."[23]

You and I, we need each other. Attachment isn't optional for those of us who walk and breathe in human skin. It's part of who we are at our genetic core, required for our survival as much as air and food and water. It's not that we can't live as independent individuals. But independence driven by fear and insecurity isn't independence at all—it's isolation. True independence finds its anchor in relationship.

This is what I needed to remember during the hours of my son's raging when I reached the end of myself and felt terrified about the adult my little boy might become. I needed him as much as he needed me. It was in relationship that we'd find our way.

A counselor once told me that wounds suffered in relationship are also healed in relationship. That's both the rub and the beauty of it. The very thing that brought us pain will be the means through which our healing will come. For Jack, he needed to learn to trust the arms of a new mom. For me, I had to learn to love in spite of the gaping holes, without retreating and slamming my heart closed.

And for both of us, we needed to dig deep to find a faith that believes even the deepest wounds can be healed by a healing God.

When human love fails, a greater love remains. A healing, filling, securing love that fills the darkest black holes. Even when we swallow up the gift and forget the beauty of the offering.

"Can a mother forget the baby at her breast and have no compassion on the child she has borne? Though she may forget, I will not forget you! See, I have engraved you on the palms of my hands."[24]

My name. Jack's name. Carved into the safety of God's hand in fat red letters.

CHAPTER 18

The Grace of a Rough Draft

As I aimed to become a teacher, God made me a student. My spirit as a questioner does not affront Him; rather, it reflects Him, and honors Him, and pulls me toward Him. Through our gifts and weaknesses, our strengths and shortcomings, He works in each life thus.

—CAROLYN WEBER, *Surprised by Oxford*

We are meant to be real, and to see and recognize the real. We are all more than we know, and that wondrous reality, that wholeness, holiness, is there for all of us, not the qualified only.

—MADELEINE L'ENGLE, *Walking on Water*

I CAME HOME FROM HIGH SCHOOL ANGRY. THE TEST SCRUNCHED in my hands. Throwing my backpack onto the floor, I flung my adolescent self onto the bed and sobbed.

I know. Hard to imagine me the drama queen. But there you have it.

My parents must've heard the commotion, because soon Mom opened my bedroom door, squeezed her head between the door and frame.

"What's wrong, honey? Bad day at school?"

I've never had much tolerance for obvious questions. So I launched into a louder and more frustrated wail. Award-worthy, people.

"I'll never be good enough. Never! No matter how hard I work, it's never enough." I threw the crumpled test to the floor.

To her credit, my mom neither laughed nor reprimanded. I'm not sure I would have shown the same mercy. Instead, as I remember it, she picked my test up off the floor and pressed flat the paper. For a moment, she didn't say anything. Just analyzed the document.

"Is this what you're upset about?"

I sniffled and nodded. Didn't she know? Couldn't she see the grade marked in ink at the top?

"It's an A minus, Michele."

I knew that. I started crying again.

She should've called in the family for a public mocking. Or doused me with a bucket of ice. Instead, she saw my heartache through the theatrics.

Against all reason, I couldn't see the A. I could only see the minus.

I'm not sure when I became a perfectionist. Perhaps I was born this way, the perfection gene delivered right along with my seven-pound, one-ounce self. Mom says I was a perfect baby, sleeping, eating, and pooping in the right order and on time. The fact that I receive this as a compliment hints at my dysfunction.

As far as birth order is concerned, I'm a typical firstborn female. Driven, high-achieving, and a fan of personal excellence.

(You saw how I did that, didn't you? I called it "excellence." We perfectionists like to come up with new names for our disorder.) That would imply my perfectionism is the result of both personality and environment. And then there's the wee little fact that I was raised by two perfectionists.

I didn't stand a chance.

So, hi. My name is Michele. And I'm a raging perfectionist. I've been in recovery for four decades, and I'm happy to report I'm slowly breaking free of panic, paranoia, and the need for everything within the silverware drawer to be perfectly aligned.

Nonetheless, perfectionism nips at my heels. If you see a typo somewhere in this book or on my blog, don't tell me about it. Or, rather, do tell me. But be gentle, positive, and infinitely affirming. Otherwise, I'm likely to throw myself on my bed and sob.

The good news is I've discovered four sure cures for perfectionism: Parenting. Marriage. Writing. And parenting.

But mostly parenting.

Being the overachiever I am, I managed to log multiple personal failures in each category before my fortieth birthday. I was a divorced, remarried, perfectionist biological mom and stepmom who made her living as a writer and just acquired three special-needs children.

Like dynamite next to an open flame, my friends. It had all the makings of a major disaster.

⁓

The note was waiting in my email inbox by the time I got home.

Moments before, I'd dropped off the twins for another afternoon of preschool. At the same time, I left two bags of snacks and drinks for later that week, my assigned date. I had to catch a flight and wouldn't be able to bring them in on the assigned day. So I took the stash in early and privately patted myself on the back.

Look how prompt you are! What a good mom you are!

I hoped all the other parents noticed. I should get a sticker.

Anxious to get started on the day's work, I drove straight home. Preschool lasted two itty-bitty hours, and I knew the time would disappear like a rabbit in a magic act. I settled at my office desk to get to work. That's when I noticed the email. From the teacher.

"It has come to my attention that a lot of snack is being brought in days and sometimes weeks before scheduled snack days, and it has become extremely difficult to remember who has snack and who doesn't. Please bring in snack on your scheduled day only."

An email blasted out to every parent on her list, including the parents I'd just seen at drop-off.

My humiliation wouldn't have been greater if I'd been forced to squat on a miniature stool in the corner. Sitting at my desk, I could feel anger bubbling up and filling my face with heat. A public reprimand, by a preschool teacher. I doubted she was old enough to have her driver's license.

Behind the outrage, I felt shame. Shame at my inability to do this mothering thing right. I couldn't even get the snack schedule down. Every day, I showed up late to school. In the evenings, I struggled to get dinner made and baths done. A coworker commented on the increasing typos in my emails, and several friends mentioned my disconnect from relationship. My boys struggled and my littles cried. Everywhere I turned, I felt like I was failing. The snack fiasco confirmed my worst fear: I was a terrible mother. *I'll never be good enough. Never! No matter how hard I work, it's never enough. Waaaaaa!*

I wrote a curt reply to the teacher, filled with plastic apologies, and then fumed for the rest of the day. Intellectually, I knew it wasn't a big deal. We're talking snack schedules, not life and death. But this public and embarrassing reprimand landed as the final straw in a camel-back-breaking string of motherly mishaps. After nearly two decades in this gig, I'd become the chronically tardy, homework-neglecting, appointment-missing, snack-schedule-disrupting mom. I was a disgrace to the position.

Parenting is easy before you become a parent. After you actually have a baby and acquire the title, you discover you can change a diaper but don't have a clue how to get the crying to stop. You can teach a child how to hold a fork, but that doesn't mean she's actually going to use it. And you can talk about stranger danger, the importance of speed limit signs, and the seriousness of choosing your friends. But that doesn't mean he'll stay away from the weird guy in the white van, drive thirty miles an hour, and hang out with the "nice Christian kids from the youth group."

If there were a championship game for the most controlling mother, there's a good chance I'd captain the team. It wasn't that I was a power freak. I just wanted my kids to make good choices, love God, and honor others. I felt the weight of responsibility to raise them to be functioning and respectful adults. And so I did what I could as a mom to help them get there.

But then we'd get a call from the school. A letter from a teacher. Unravel a mess or a lie. Find illegal fireworks in a bedroom. Every wrong turn and bad choice, if I followed them like a trail of bread crumbs, led back to me.

What kind of mother would let this happen? Where did I go wrong?

Irrational, yes. But perfectionism isn't rational. It's poison.

The first major blow against my infernal perfectionism happened in the ten-by-ten-foot home of an African woman named Macey.

We sat in the darkness of her shack, a lean-to with dirt floor, mud-brick walls, and scraps of sheet metal propped up as the roof. A thin scarf wrapped her head to tie at the base of her neck. In spite of the sun filtering through open door and window spaces, she pulled her sweater tight around her shoulders.

She had AIDS. Of course, she never admitted as much; the shame kept her quiet. Instead, she labeled it tuberculosis, likely the truth, at least in part. But I knew AIDS to be the disease behind the disease.

This was our third or fourth visit in the course of a two-week mission trip. In bits and pieces, over hours and through a translator, Macey shared her story. A single mom raising a son. Unemployed, unable to work. Terminally ill. Her husband left a year or two before, choosing another wife and family, leaving her sick and without any means to raise and feed her eleven-year-old boy. Her eyes bled grief.

I knew the story, felt the ache of familiarity. Ten years before, a counselor, John, recognized the similar despair in me. My first marriage was weeks from ending, and I knew I could do nothing to resurrect it. Twenty-seven and with an infant son, I'd failed in the most profound way. My life was over, and I didn't think I could go on.

Determined to resurrect a dwindling spark, John cracked open the thick book in his lap and started to read:

He has sent me to bind up the brokenhearted . . .
to bestow on them a crown of beauty
instead of ashes,
the oil of joy

instead of mourning,
and a garment of praise
instead of a spirit of despair.
They will be called oaks of righteousness,
a planting of the LORD
for the display of his splendor.[25]

"God is not finished with you yet, Michele." He looked at me with an intensity birthed of deep belief. "Someday you will be an oak of righteousness, a planting of the Lord for the display of his splendor!"

I heard his words, the words of Isaiah 61, but couldn't receive them. It seemed too good to be true. I couldn't believe such a gift. Couldn't believe it could be given to a wreck of a woman like me.

Until Macey. Until ten years later when I sat across from a broken African woman, no longer a broken woman myself, and understood the miracle of Isaiah's offering.

Feeling the urgency, I handed Macey a Sosotho Bible. This would be our last visit, a Bible in her language a parting gift. Then, with it sitting on her lap, I cracked open the pages and thumbed through until I found book, chapter, and verse. After pointing to her page, I opened my own and read Isaiah 61 aloud for both of us to hear.

"A crown of beauty instead of ashes, the oil of joy instead of mourning.... They will be called oaks of righteousness, a planting of the LORD for the display of his splendor."

I leaned forward over the pages to pour forward the offering I'd received so many years before.

"God isn't finished with you yet, Macey! He has a plan for you. For your son. If God could bring beauty from the ashes of my life, he can do the same for you. I believe it!"

Even as I said the words, I could feel the nod of God's head and hear his whisper: *I told you so.*

I was like a blind man finally able to see; God opened my eyes. If I'd come to Macey with only my perfection—a neat and fairytale life—I would've had absolutely nothing to offer. Instead, I came broken, flawed. A divorced, former single mother who thought she'd fallen too far out of the reach of salvation's hand. Who didn't yet understand that only a marred life gives birth to the most beautiful redemption.

Right there, as I was humbled by poverty, both Macey's and mine, God helped me see the miracle of the exchange.

Beauty for ashes. Gladness for mourning. Praise for despair.

Author Madeleine L'Engle said, "An artist at work is in a condition of complete and total faith."[26] As a writer, every time I sit down to write, I trust the page to transform my random and rough words into something worthy. Even so, I know it starts with a draft, an ugly and imperfect collection of words and stories that don't yet say what they're supposed to say.

Perfectionism has no place in writing. I know this. It's an art form honed through failure more than success. Likewise, I'm learning perfectionism has no place in living either. Just as a writer must embrace a rough draft as the necessary means to a book's successful end, I had to learn how to embrace my life's process. Including the countless ways my shortcomings and flaws have made me a better character in my own story.

Life must be lived with a writer's courage. Just as a blank page cannot be improved, nothing can be done with an unlived, untried life. To dare to live will involve mistakes and missteps. You and I will end up with choices we regret, opportunities we missed, words we wish we could go back and say or leave unsaid.

Perfection is impossible. But a rough draft, no matter how flawed, sits within reach of an artist's redemption.

My friend Rabbi Evan Moffic recently wrote words so beautiful and true I wrapped them around me like a blanket: "The broken and the whole live together. They both shape who we are. No life is perfect. We have our highs and lows, our moments of shattered pieces and of divine inspiration. Together they make us a human being, created in the image of God. Together they make us holy."[27]

This is the grace—the holiness—of a rough-draft life. Of children who struggle and parents who fail. Of broken marriages and disappointing A minuses. Of trying and stumbling, but finding the grace to get up and try again.

The preschool teacher eventually wrote me back regarding the snack-schedule fiasco. She explained, contrary to my interpretation, that her reprimand wasn't directed at me. I might have overreacted. What a shocker.

Soon after, we met face-to-face. Sitting in small, preschool chairs made for buns half the size of my own, I told her our family's story, how overnight we'd become mom and dad to three littles, and how I was still struggling to find my footing in the midst of such upheaval. Rather than judge, condemn, or offer advice, she delivered understanding and lots of grace. Even gave me special permission to bring our snacks in early if needed.

Simply, she allowed me a cushion of space to live this crazy, rough-draft life of mine one day at a time. In the process, she helped me offer myself the same grace.

I will probably always feel driven to be the best mom I can be. It's part of my DNA, that whole firstborn pursuit of "excellence." But now I also feel driven to forgive myself my many failings. To endure the missed appointments, tardy slips, and forgotten homework on occasion. Not because I don't care. But because I know I won't always get it right.

This is a rough-draft life. And whatever I didn't like about today, I can always edit tomorrow.

CHAPTER 19

Dying in the Deep

The time when there is nothing at all in your soul except a cry for help may be just the time when God can't give it: you are like the drowning man who can't be helped because he clutches and grabs.

—C. S. LEWIS, *A Grief Observed*

Not till we are lost . . . do we begin to find ourselves.

—HENRY DAVID THOREAU, *Walden*

EIGHTY FEET UNDER THE SURFACE OF THE OCEAN.

Somewhere off the coast of Playa del Carmen, Mexico, Troy and I went scuba diving in blue-green water as clear as crystal.

It should've been the time of my life. A last-minute, grown-up vacation. The kids were a thousand miles away, in Colorado with my parents. For the first time in too long, we had eight days together, alone.

So we went scuba diving, something we'd done together countless times. Our descent had begun five or ten minutes before, the two of us along with Alberto, an expert dive master. We'd moved a foot or two at a time, releasing air from our BCDs (buoyancy control devices) and equalizing our ears until we'd settled close to the bottom, negotiating buoyancy to hover above the ocean floor.

Spread out in front of us sat the Santa Rosa. In more than eleven years of diving, it's my favorite of all the reefs. We'd decided to do it a second time because we'd never forgotten our awe at the first, years before. Just as we'd remembered, the living coral teemed with sea life. Angelfish. Yellow tang. Needlefish. Schools of grouper. Massive barracuda. Countless varieties decorated the water with vibrant color pulled straight from an artist's palette.

The dive started off level, with the ocean floor and reef below. Then the Santa Rosa turned vertical, becoming a steep wall that plunged into a black abyss, depths unknown. In spite of high visibility, I couldn't see the bottom. It sat at a depth far beyond human sight. This made the Santa Rosa dive both exhilarating and intimidating, hovering as we were over the dark unknown. It made me thankful for my BCD and the remaining bubbles of air inside, the only thing keeping me from a long and fatal sinking.

For this particular dive, we'd hover right around eighty feet, examine the reef, and take in the marine life. We'd stay far away from the black unknown and instead allow the current to take us to our pickup location.

Everything seemed fine for the first several minutes. At the surface, I'd had some trouble with my mask. As I prepped to tuck-and-roll from the boat into the water, the strap broke. While I balanced on the edge, weighted down with a full tank and gear, the boat captain grabbed me another.

Untried equipment is always risky, but the new mask appeared to be working fine. No leaking or fogging. The oceanic panorama couldn't have been more clear. A relief. Mask trouble can ruin a good dive.

It happened the moment we settled into formation and

started drifting with the current. Without explanation, my heart started to race. The beats came faster and faster, like a gas pedal stuck to the floor. It made no sense. I wasn't in any danger. Still, my heart pounded like a judge's gavel on his desk, whack after whack in a futile attempt to gain order.

Thump-thump! Thump-thump! Thump-thump!

With every screaming beat, I felt more out of control. My throat tightened. I couldn't breathe. The wetsuit seemed to shrink tight around my neck, the air in my throat thick. My regulator continued to churn out oxygen, and I continued to inhale and exhale, albeit in spasmodic motions. But the air didn't seem to make it to my lungs. I felt out of breath and sucked in big gulps of air in frantic desperation.

I can't breathe! Dear God, I can't breathe!

I reached for my regulator, feeling the impulse to yank it from my mouth and stop the choking sensation. An irrational temptation, I knew that. The only thing keeping me alive was the tank strapped to my back and hose running into my mouth.

I'd been diving for more than a decade. I knew the routine, had done the same type of dive countless times. But this time was different. Whether it was the racing heart or lack of air, I wasn't thinking clearly. Logic kept the regulator in place, but the unyielding urge to pull it out remained. It was as if someone else had taken over and started calling the shots.

Thump-thump! Thump-thump! Thump-thump!

My heart continued to race so fast and hard I thought I could hear its echo like sonar in the water. Like a soundtrack to a horror movie.

I considered shooting to the surface, inflating my BCD, and going straight to the fresh air at the top. A death sentence, I knew. At eighty feet down, the water pressure is so great that the organs—heart, lungs—shrink. The air contracts, pulls in. To shoot to the surface without giving the body time to adjust and expand, slowly, would burst my insides like an overinflated balloon.

God, help! I'm going to drown!

Both water and regulator muffled my screams. I was dying, but no one knew. I flipped around in the water, flailing arms and fins, the water turning my panicky movements into slow motion. Scanning the sea, I searched for my husband, my dive buddy. He'd know what to do.

But I couldn't find him. In spite of my flailing—or maybe because of it—I couldn't see his familiar blue fins and neon yellow mask strap through the deep dark of my panic.

This is it. I'm going to die.

I remember the irony of that thought. After more than a year of fearing death by cancer, I would now succumb to an ocean. It didn't seem fair, to survive one horror only to die by another.

Then Alberto appeared. The dive master.

To this day, I don't know what brought him to my side. Don't know how he knew he was about to lose one of his team. He just showed up, out of nowhere, and hovered with me, eighty feet under the ocean, in my panic.

With a glance at my bulging eyes, he knew something was wrong. He took quick inventory of my tank, regulator, and other equipment. When all appeared to be working, he took my hands in his. Held both tight.

Embarrassed, I tried to pull away, pointed to the surface as my signal to abandon the dive.

He wouldn't release me. Instead, holding my hands tight, he looked at me. Using one hand, he pointed to his eyes. Then to my eyes. Then back to his eyes. He held on, showing no signs of panic and never turning his eyes from my own.

In all, my first panic attack lasted no more than ten minutes. While Alberto held my eyes and my hands, my heart rate returned to normal. When he was convinced I would not die on his watch, he released me and we continued our dive along the Santa Rosa wall. It was just as exquisite as I remembered it.

It was weeks before I understood what had happened during those precarious minutes buried in the Caribbean Ocean. It took a little research and the help of a counselor to wrap my mind around it and give it a name.

But this I knew for sure. I wouldn't have survived the Santa Rosa if it weren't for my dive master.

He never said a word, but he refused to let me go.

⁓

A few years ago, a good friend and coworker, Danny de Armas, served me up a slice of wisdom I still chew on from time to time: "We all pray for a harvest, for God to give the blessing of bounty," he said, through the phone. "But when the harvest comes and he gives us everything we've asked for, we complain. It's easy to forget that harvest is a whole lot of work."

Our diving trip to Mexico came in the middle of a season of harvest.

About the same time the children came, years of professional seed-planting came to fruition. Troy's business, in its eighth year, had grown multiple times over, requiring him to work late nights and many Saturdays. My career experienced similar growth. Speaking engagements, coaching clients, writing contracts. I couldn't explain the influx: I'd neglected my career when cancer and kids entered the picture. And yet that's when the phone started ringing.

For both of us, this is what we'd been dreaming of and working for. Two self-employed business owners hoping to help our babies fly. The irony? We'd planned to be empty nesters when it happened. Not middle-aged parents of three littles.

Thus, the rub. Family was, and always has been, the priority. We knew our children needed our attention and investment, perhaps the littles even more than the bigs. But we also felt the tug of our dreams, the gift of open doors. And the weight of providing for a household that had nearly doubled. Were these opportunities evidence of God's financial provision?

Welcome to the Cushatt family juggling act. Two parents, two careers. And six high-needs, always-moving children.

That fall, in an attempt to embrace our harvest, I traveled every weekend for two solid months. On weekdays, after flying home from one coast or the other, I unpacked my suitcase, rolled up my sleeves, and dove right into my role as wife and mom. Cooking meals, signing field-trip forms, driving carpool, helping with homework. Not to mention catching up on the office work I'd missed. Come Thursday or Friday, I'd wake well before dawn, load a newly packed suitcase into my car, and head back to Denver International Airport.

The travel, new relationships, and opportunities both honored and exhilarated me. It was a harvest, and I gave thanks for the bounty. It came when we needed it, but also when I least expected it. And, after a year of fighting cancer, parenting teenagers, and learning to love wounded littles, when I could least manage it.

Sometime late September, Troy noticed signs of my unraveling. Like an overdrawn bank account, I'd spent more than I'd brought in for far too long. I was physically and emotionally bankrupt. It wasn't that I was unhappy with my life. I just didn't know how to keep up with it. And the not-keeping-up made me feel like I was failing. And the feeling-like-a-failure drained energy and emotion I didn't have to spare.

Troy could see my atypical exhaustion. Truth was, his schedule had been equally as demanding, and he felt much the same. So he booked an inexpensive trip to a Caribbean beach, just the two of us. One week of quiet and rest and sleep. My parents, God bless them, offered to fly in from Nevada to watch the kids. I didn't know quite how that would work out—two sweet and untried grandparents with the Destroyers of All Things Valuable. But I didn't care, couldn't afford to. I knew I was days from epic collapse.

On a Thursday in October, after I finished one last speaking engagement, I emptied one suitcase and packed another. This one filled with shorts, swimming suit, and absolutely no responsibilities.

For the first two days of our vacation, I did nothing but sleep and eat. I woke up whenever the urge struck me. Ate when I felt hungry. Slept when my eyes would no longer stay open. From late morning until sunset, I lay beneath palm trees and didn't move.

After a couple of days, I rose from my coma.

Then the Santa Rosa. My descent into the deep. And the panic that almost kept me there.

Jesus' disciples knew all about water, waves, and the terror of a possible drowning. At least four grew up on the Sea of Galilee, fishermen who knew how to watch the clouds and save their necks.

So when Jesus suggested an innocent, "Let's go over to the other side of the lake," they jumped aboard the boat and set sail toward the far shore.[28] They'd done this a hundred times before.

But they didn't expect the storm. A "squall," Luke says, fierce and consuming. One moment everything was fine, the next the boat was about to capsize. These were experienced fishermen, more qualified than most in navigating an unexpected storm. But this wasn't an ordinary storm.

Thump-thump! Thump-thump! Thump-thump!

Terror coursed through the veins of every boat passenger who wasn't divine. Peter. James. Matthew. John. Twelve friends and Jesus-followers in a boat about to go under.

Oh, God, help! "We're going to drown!"[29]

I imagine the storm muffled their screams. Undisturbed, Jesus slept. His breathing and his body rhythmic and sure. No gasps or panic, no reaching or grabbing. Only peace.

His disregard of their terror seems heartless at best, cruel at worst. How could Jesus remain unruffled, unsympathetic? I'm sure his divinity and relationship with the maker of the waves provided him a unique perspective, an awareness of God that calmed frayed nerves.

But his humanness would've felt fear too. A heart beating out of control, breaths coming too quick, a tight chest and frantic eyes.

Even so, faced with the same furious squall, Jesus remained at peace while his companions writhed in panic.

Why? What made the difference?

This was the question I needed answered, eighty feet under the ocean and every day above it. I've lived long enough to know that unexpected squalls are part of the deal. Just because the sun is shining in the morning doesn't mean you'll see it in the afternoon. This life is unpredictable and, at times, terrifying. But I'm tired of the fear and bouncing up and down with every unexpected wave. I want to know the secret to sleeping in the boat.

Jesus answered my question with a question of his own.

"Where is your faith?"

These are his only recorded words to a nearly drowned, still-trembling band of followers. I can't help but wonder if, in that four-word question, we have the secret to a peace that rises above the waves.

Where is my faith?

When cancer rocked my boat, my faith was in my ability to predict the ultimate outcome. In doctors' words and test results. In my ability to manage my pain, eat organic food, and keep the cancer from recurring.

When my son decided to choose a life contrary to our beliefs and values, my faith was in my ability to talk him out of his foolishness, to strong-arm his choices and deliver ultimatums. To will him into becoming the man I wanted him to be.

When three grieving littles were added to my home, my faith was in my supermom ability to fix them, heal them, and make up for all their horrific losses. To be their savior and deliverer of hope.

Where is my faith? In myself, more often than not. Which is why an unexpected squall—every last one of them over the span of two years—unraveled me. A boat anchored to itself is not anchored at all.

Shoring up your faith in the right place is far more important than simply claiming to have it. If I believe only in what I can see, manage, and control, sooner or later something will come along to rock my boat. When that happens, I'll scream into the wind, "I'm going to drown!"

Instead, I must secure my faith where it cannot be unmoored. In the one who controls the waves and whose peace runs so deep we can find a way to sleep in the storm. My faith belongs there, with him. That's the secret sauce between panic and peace.

"But we have this treasure in jars of clay to show that this all-surpassing power is from God and not from us. We are hard pressed on every side, but not crushed; perplexed, but not in despair; persecuted, but not abandoned; struck down, but not destroyed.... So we fix our eyes not on what is seen, but on what is unseen, since what is seen is temporary, but what is unseen is eternal."[30]

Faith is choosing the anchor of your focus. It's about turning your eyes away from the questions that lead to fear, and instead locking eyes with the one who knows the answers.

Like a dive master who soothes a girl's panic eighty feet under the ocean.

A part of me died that day, next to the Santa Rosa, deep in the Caribbean Ocean. Faced with my frailty and exhausted from fighting wind and waves of a life I hadn't expected, I had to die to the self-sufficiency and arrogance that had fooled me into thinking I could do all, be all, without consequence. That I could anchor myself to my own boat and not pay the price.

Thank God. He looked me in the eye, and he refused to let me go.

CHAPTER 20

Lay It Down

Suffering is unbearable if you aren't certain that God is for you and with you.

—TIMOTHY KELLER, *Walking with God through Pain and Suffering*

When I let God fight for me, He always wins.

—BO STERN, *Ruthless: Knowing the God Who Fights for You*

"I'M THINKING ABOUT TAKING THE KIDS SKIING TOMORROW." HE announced it. Not a question up for discussion, but a statement of fact.

"What? Without me?" I'm a bit sensitive to rejection. You know, not a fan of being the lone girl not asked to the prom. I might have pouted.

My husband, bless him, scrambled to explain. "I thought you could have a whole day to yourself."

An entire day? I didn't expect that but liked the sound of it. I couldn't remember the last time I'd had a day to myself at home. Even when the littles went to school, I still had one or two big kids loitering on the premises. Apparently twelve noon is a perfectly acceptable time for a twenty-year-old to start his day.

I didn't want to miss out on a family adventure, but the thought of a quiet day was a slice of goodness too sweet to pass up.

The following morning, Troy loaded kids and ski gear into the car and pulled out of the driveway before 7:00 a.m. Then, like a banker counting his coins, I catalogued the precious hours until their return. At least ten. Maybe twelve if he ran into traffic.

Dear God, bringeth traffic.

It didn't take long to plot out my time. First, a rare indulgence. In yoga pants and a ball cap, I drove to Lamar's Donuts to pick up a chocolate-covered, Bavarian-cream-filled long john. Go big or go home, I say. Taking my prize home, I poured a mug of Starbucks Caffe Verona (is there any more worthy roast?), snuggled in front of a dancing fireplace, and cracked the cover of a new book.

For almost two hours I didn't move. Bliss, I tell you. Some of you believe the Feast of Heaven will involve grand dining-room tables, roasted turkeys and lamb shanks, and side dishes and chandeliers galore. But at my eternal feast, there will be platters of donuts, bottomless cups of dark-roast coffee, and loungers.

In typical form, the day passed too quickly. I read two different books. Took a short nap. Made dinner. Soaked in a bubble bath. A quiet, crisis-free day. Exactly what my overtired, overstressed self needed.

Which is why I wasn't at all prepared for another panic attack.

It started midafternoon in the master bathroom. While looking in the mirror, I felt something underneath my tongue. A bump, no bigger than the head of a pencil, where all those blasted surgeries had taken place. Something where nothing had been before.

In the span of seconds, an alarm went off in my head.

No, please no. I stared at myself in the mirror. The pain had increased over the past two weeks. But I tried to shake free the worry, knowing pain didn't always equate to cancer. In fact, a few weeks before, I'd had my two-year PET scan. The results had come back in a few days. Negative. No cancer.

This was big news. To get a NED two years post–oral cancer meant I'd passed the biggest mile marker. Five years was still the magic number, but most recurrences happened within the first two. I had every reason to celebrate. So why the panic?

My heart pounded out of my chest. I could see my hands shaking as I brushed my hair and tried to continue with the day. As if I wasn't losing my mind.

Get ahold of yourself, Michele.

Against all reason, I was losing my grip on reality. But what about the bump, and the low-level pain that had grown worse over the previous weeks? Maybe there really was something going on. Maybe the cancer had come back.

My heart continued to race. Nausea cramped my insides. I could hear the pounding in my ears, feel the tightness in my throat.

I looked at the clock. A little past three. It would still be a few hours until Troy and the kids came home. I was spiraling fast, didn't know if I could make it. Like watching myself on a movie screen, I could see it happening but could do nothing to make it stop. I tried praying, but I couldn't seem to focus my words or thoughts. Instead, I paced from room to room, searching for a big enough diversion to interrupt the panic. Nothing.

I needed Troy. He could talk me off my ledge.

I found my phone and dialed his number. By some miracle, he picked up.

"Hey, babe."

At the sound of his voice, I burst into tears. The familiarity of him, the safety, released the anxiety and pressure that threatened to split me in two.

"I need you," I cried. "I don't know what's happening. But it feels like that day in Mexico. Under the ocean. I'm afraid."

My words came out in staccato beats, between breaths and sobs. Did he think I was crazy? Was I?

"I'm sorry, hon—what happened?"

I told him about the bump in my mouth, about the way it broke open and bled and my fear that the cancer had come back.

"I can't do it again. I just can't do another surgery." I continued to cry into the phone, borrowing trouble from the what-ifs of tomorrow. Of course, if I had to do it all over again, I would. We don't have a choice about these things. But in that moment, on the phone, I exposed my deepest fear: that I'd have to endure the pain and fear and unknowns all over again.

"You're going to be okay, Michele." He said it with such confidence, such unwavering belief. I wanted to believe him.

"Tell me again. Please. I need to hear it." Again he whispered reassurances to me. Not promises that everything would turn out exactly like I wanted it. But assurances that, regardless of what was to come, I would be okay. And he'd be with me. Then he prayed, I prayed, and I turned the fear and unknown back over to God. For the millionth time.

Minutes later, we hung up. For the two hours until he pulled back into the driveway, it was enough.

~

This wasn't the last time my anxiety interfered with my living.

It happened once more, only two weeks later. This time I traveled out-of-state for a speaking engagement. At night, after

I'd settled in a hotel room eight hundred miles away from home, anxiety ripped me awake and wouldn't let me alone for almost two hours.

In forty years, I'd never experienced anything like it. Divorce had brought a measure of grief and depression. To be expected. But never a strangling anxiety that kept me from ordinary life. It hit without warning, escalating in minutes and incapacitating for much longer. My body no longer felt my own.

As long as I'm confessing, I'll make one more shameful admission: I'd typically assumed that those who claimed anxiety and panic attacks fabricated their experiences. It seemed more a shortcut for attention than an authentic event. Can't control your thoughts? Get more sleep. Feeling anxious, agitated? Go for a walk or run, maybe take a nap or chat with a counselor. Don't let a diagnosis become a cop-out for poor coping skills, I thought.

Until I couldn't "skill" my way through. Me, a type-A, in-control go-getter who rarely met a challenge she couldn't beat. Except for this. I couldn't beat it.

My years in the medical field wired me up to take a more holistic approach to physical and mental health. For almost twenty years, I ran or biked a minimum of four or five times a week. I went to Pilates and yoga classes and took long walks in Colorado's open space. I avoided fast food and processed food and cooked almost all our meals at home with fresh ingredients. From a spiritual standpoint, I read my Bible daily, completed countless studies, participated in a handful of small groups, and attended church every weekend.

Check. Check. Check. I'd done all the critical to-do's.

I do believe healthy lifestyle habits have a huge impact on mental health and quality of life. Food, exercise, spirituality, positive self-talk, and quality relationships impact our emotional and physical health far more than we realize. In many cases, these lifestyle habits can elevate mood, change perspective, and renew energy.

But I also learned, the hard way, that sometimes trauma grows beyond a long walk's ability to cure. The losses, crises, transitions, and upheavals extend beyond the arms' capacity to hold. At times, even when your belief in and love of God run strong and true, your body just can't take any more of the trauma.

This is what I saw in my littles. Dinner, a good night's sleep, and consistent Sunday school attendance weren't going to cure them of their attachment wounds, their loss of a mom and dad. They needed years of therapy, agonizing work in building trust relationships, and maybe medical intervention. Time would tell.

Though I was reluctant to admit it, I started to see that the same could be said of me. After the joint traumas of cancer, struggling adolescents, and addition of three special-needs children, my forty-year-old body began to shut down. Physiologically, I'd pushed myself to the very edge of capacity. A long nap or vacation wasn't going to solve the problem. In fact, only when I slowed down and stopped moving did the lurking brokenness get my undivided attention.

On vacation with my husband.

During a full day of quiet in my house.

And sleeping alone in a hotel room.

When the cacophony of my life silenced, my body screamed.

"It's simply been too much, Michele."

Bev, the counselor and leadership mentor I'd seen off and on for two years, sat across from me with nothing but empathy lighting her features.

"But I have a good life!" I protested. "It's not like I'm depressed or sad. I love my life!"

"I believe you," she reassured. "But it's a full life. You've had more than your share of stress over the past two years. And your brain is maxed out."

Her words made sense, but still I resisted. This seemed one more in a never-ending string of personal failures.

"Everyone has stuff to deal with. I'm not the only one. So why does it seem like everyone else manages it okay and I can't? What's wrong with me?"

That, right there, was the question I'd been asking myself for two years. What did I do to cause cancer? Why didn't the cyst go away? Why were my boys struggling? Why couldn't I figure out how to help my littles heal?

What's wrong with me?

"Did you hear what you just said?" she asked, stopping me in my self-talk.

"What?"

"You just said, 'What's wrong with me?'" She waited, let that sink in. "You expect a lot of yourself."

I did. But I thought I was supposed to. That's what a good, hardworking, Jesus-loving girl does. She gets her act together and pushes herself to be the best she can be. Holiness requires high expectations, right?

"Maybe you're not supposed to manage all this. Maybe, instead, you're supposed to experience it. Walk through it. Do the best you can."

There's a thought. I didn't know what to say.

"Allowing yourself frailty is one of the kindest things you can do for yourself." Again she waited, allowed me to absorb her words.

"Before the cancer and children, you already had a full life. A husband, three boys, a career. Plenty of opportunities for crises right there."

She took a breath, continued.

"Then cancer. Followed closely by three high-needs children. You layered those right on top of your already full life and expected yourself to function just the same."

True. I'd done that. Because I thought that's what I was supposed to do.

"But you can't do it all. You can do more than most, I'll give you that. But even you have your limits."

Why did that last part sound like a personal flaw? Limits sounded like lackings.

"You need to let some things go. And not feel guilty about it."

Was she reading my mind?

"And one more thing. You're not going to like it."

She caught my eye, made sure I met hers. I braced myself.

"I want you to call your doctor. I think you need a prescription, something for anxiety. Your brain needs help to heal from all this."

And the final nail in my coffin of self-loathing sank into place.

~

Within hours of leaving her office, I contacted my primary doctor. But it took weeks for me to relinquish my shame.

I couldn't deny I'd reached the end of myself. I had no more tricks up my sleeve, no special powers I could pull from my red cape. The stress and exhaustion had taken every last bit of me. A vacation or an afternoon nap wasn't going to fix what was broken.

I'd been beaten. Utterly and completely. I couldn't strap on hiking boots and conquer this mountain. Couldn't Bible study my way into an energy boost. Couldn't overcome my exhaustion with increased church attendance. I still ran, ate healthy, slept seven or eight hours at night. But like emptying a thimble of water in desert sand, it wasn't nearly enough to make new life grow.

I kept thinking a better woman wouldn't have spiraled so easily. Someone who really loves Jesus—whose faith runs authentic and deep—would've faced cancer with courage and without fear. A selfless and sacrificial mother would've poured herself out on behalf of three hurting children, day after day, without wanting to run away.

And a strong woman, a worthy one, wouldn't need a pill to cope with ordinary life.

At least, this is what I kept telling myself. The reason I kept berating myself. Until God delivered absolution in an unexpected place.

In the Old Testament book of 2 Chronicles sits the story of King Jehoshaphat. I usually skip over any biblical accounts with names I can't pronounce. But this one hid a jewel.

"Some people came and told Jehoshaphat, 'A vast army is coming against you from Edom. . . .' Alarmed, Jehoshaphat resolved to inquire of the Lord, and he proclaimed a fast for all Judah."[31]

That caught my attention for two reasons. First, the words "vast army." I knew a thing or two about circumstances of cosmic proportions. "Alarmed" about sums it up. And second, he prayed. "Jehoshaphat resolved to inquire of the Lord," before digging into his stash of chocolate, getting a pedicure, or going back to bed. A man who faced a vast army and fell to his knees deserved my attention.

His prayer, recorded in the verses that follow, is exquisite. I love his boldness and honesty. The way he acknowledges God's authority while simultaneously recounting the unfortunate details of his predicament. But what I love most is the humility that ends his petition: "For we have no power to face this vast army that is attacking us. We do not know what to do, but our eyes are upon you."[32]

In two sentences, the King of Judah looks outside himself for help. He takes the crown off his own head and puts it squarely on the only one who deserves to wear it.

It's beautiful. One of the most powerful pictures in the Bible, in my humble opinion.

On cue, a prophet comes forward to deliver a message, God's response to Jehoshaphat's prayer.

"Do not be afraid or discouraged because of this vast army. For the battle is not yours, but God's."[33]

These verses became my rescue, far more than the medication or counsel. You see, I'd been fighting a battle that wasn't mine to fight. Alarmed by my vast army, I raised my shield and wielded my sword, assuming all responsibility for victory. I tried to be warrior, mother, manager, scheduler, and deity. It's no surprise I came undone.

I've long held unrealistic expectations for myself, inhuman standards, and then judged myself according to how I met—or didn't meet—them. Performance is a load far too heavy to carry, I know that now. A load I was never meant to bear.

Jesus said, "Come to me, all you who are weary and burdened, and I will give you rest. Take my yoke upon you and learn from me, for I am gentle and humble in heart, and you will find rest for your souls. For my yoke is easy and my burden is light."[34]

It was as if he said the words for me, as if Matthew penned them two thousand years ago so one day, the road-weary twenty-first-century Michele who spent a lifetime trying to meet impossible expectations would finally realize she carried an unnecessary burden.

Time to lay it down. Like Jehoshaphat with his face and crown to the ground, I relinquished the battle. It wasn't mine to fight; all along, it'd been his.

Would the cancer come back? Only he knew. But he'd be with me.

Would my boys grow up to be responsible men of integrity? Time would tell. But even now, God was on it. I didn't need to worry; I needed only to let go.

Would my littles, the children I never expected but now couldn't imagine my life without, find healing? Would they learn to trust me and overcome the trauma that had marked their past? And would they remain with our family forever?

Unanswerable questions, every last one. I was powerless. But as I stood on the front lines of these alarming battles, I heard the words of an Old Testament prophet: "Take up your positions; stand firm and see the deliverance the LORD will give you.... Do not be afraid; do not be discouraged. Go out to face them tomorrow, and the LORD will be with you."[35]

Hallelujah, God would be with me. The next day and the next and the next. It took time to unlearn my insufferable independence and self-sufficiency. I thought them to be noble qualities, proof of worth. But I'd missed the pride and insecurity that often festered as a result. Not to mention the isolation. Then self-sufficiency became nothing but foolishness.

A family can't absorb three more children without help. Thus the reason God puts us in communities and even churches of flesh-and-blood people committed to share life. I needed help, of the daily kind, to help us manage a household filled with three new special-needs children. If the church is going to advocate for the orphan, then she ought also to advocate for the families who take them in.

But learning to lean isn't just for mamas taking in extra children. It's for the woman alone in a marriage falling apart. The childless couple who, for years now, have wanted nothing more than to grow a family. The unemployed family about to lose their home to foreclosure. And, heaven forbid, the widow learning to live her life without her husband.

For me, laying down my independence began with saying it out loud: admitting a need and asking for help. First a part-time college student to help with homework after school, only a few hours a week. Then a beautiful woman, Carla, who cleaned our house and prayed over our family as she did so. And yes, taking anti-anxiety medication for a season while my body and brain recovered from the war I'd waged. Even that was an ask for help.

The beautiful thing? I discovered life is far more beautiful—and endurable—when you don't have to do it alone. Timothy Keller says it this way: "There is no way you will be able to grow spiritually apart from a deep involvement in a community of other believers. You can't live the Christian life without a band of Christian friends, without a family of believers in which you find a place."[36]

In the relinquishing of independence, I discovered community. My brokenness gave me connection, relationship. I thought asking for help was an admission of weakness. Instead, I discovered it a declaration of strength. Like King Jehoshaphat, it was in the laying down of my crown that I finally found my place.

With so many broken and beautiful others, each of us hanging on the promises of God.

Our God is a refuge for the broken, not a shelf for the display of the shiny. No more pride for those who have it all together, or shame for those who don't.

Only stripped-bare humility, crowns on the ground. Together.

CHAPTER 21

Marker on My Walls

I don't know what's more exhausting about parenting: the getting up early, or acting like you know what you're doing.

—JIM GAFFIGAN, *Dad Is Fat*

Perfectionism means that you try desperately not to leave so much mess to clean up. But clutter and mess show us that life is being lived.

—ANNE LAMOTT, *Bird by Bird*

I STEPPED AWAY FOR A MOMENT. NOT A SMART MOVE, CONSIDERing my wealth of parental experience. Call it a lack of practice.

I'd forgotten the mother of all mothering rules: Don't leave small children unsupervised. Ever.

"You can sit and color while I get a little work done. Okay?" I smiled as I passed out new coloring books and a Ziploc bag filled with fat crayons and markers. What's better than a crisp new coloring book? Three little heads nodded and smiled in return.

Precious!

Confident they'd sit and color for a half hour (I could laugh as I write this), I left them in happy land and headed to my office. I had work to do, and I hadn't yet negotiated the how-to of a career while mothering a new passel of monkeys. In the months since Christmas, I'd fallen way behind.

I sat at my desk and replied to emails, crafted to-do lists. With the French doors open, I could hear the sound of little voices, one room away, chattering about their in-progress masterpieces.

"I'm drawing a wace car. Vwooom!"

"Mine's a rainbow!"

"Pink is my favorite color. What's yours?"

Sweet. Musical, even. I'd forgotten how children's voices could make a heart sing. God bless them. Snarky, adolescent-boy voices didn't stir up the same kind of song.

Thirty minutes later (ahem, maybe an hour), I walked back to the dining room to check in on their art. I didn't find any littles creating masterpieces. Instead, the coloring books sat abandoned. Crayons and markers littered the floor. And, to my horror, an unexpected masterpiece spanned my dining room wall.

Red, blue, and pink marker. Slashed across drywall and trim.

Blast it. I'd forgotten the second of all mothering rules: Don't give preschoolers markers. Ever.

At this point, my heart song took on a different tone.

"Who did this?" I marched out of the dining room searching for suspects. I wasn't using my happy voice. They peeked around a kitchen corner, eyes round and unblinking.

"Who colored on the walls?" I demanded, hands on hips. This is the go-to maternal stance when a crime has been committed.

Silence. None were eager to assume responsibility when the crazy woman in front of them had grown horns and a sharp, pointy tail.

So I waited. Interrogated them with glaring eyes and flintlike face. It took only a few seconds for two to turn on the third.

"It was Peanut."

Aha! I knew it. I turned my attention to the littlest of the littles. The tiny, thirty-four-pound Wielder of Destructive Forces. And then I launched the question every mother asks and no child knows how to answer: "What were you thinking?!"

She stared at me wide-eyed, stuck out her bottom lip.

"You weren't thinking, that's what." Another dose of motherly brilliance. "In this house, we color in coloring books and on paper. Not on walls."

I went to the kitchen and grabbed a wet dishcloth. "You need to clean it up. Right now." I wanted her to feel the sting of consequence so she wouldn't do the same again.

If only it were that easy.

From the moment the littles joined our family, mishaps became a daily occurrence. A week or two after the marker on my dining room walls, the same girl found an overlooked pair of scissors in a kitchen drawer and gave herself a haircut—and by haircut I mean she obliterated every evidence of her bangs. By the end of the first month, the binding and hardcover of every child's Bible we owned had been torn off and shredded. Toys, books, and DVDs likewise were broken, ripped, and snapped in two. It was as if the littles couldn't resist the urge to destroy whatever they touched.

They pulled dresser drawers off their tracks. Slammed and broke bedroom doors. Shattered shower doors. Stretched and snapped window blinds and cords. They acted more like two- and three-year-olds at times; bloody noses and potty accidents happened with alarming frequency. Not to mention the lying, manipulation, crying, and defiance that accompanied the physical damage.

"It was an accident," they said, again and again, with open hands holding the broken pieces like an offering.

These mishaps were only the barest beginning of our mess. Everything about my life felt in disarray. The frantic schedule and never-ending to-do lists. The cooking, cleaning, grocery shopping, laundering, bed making, bathing, sandwich making, dressing, hair brushing, and shoe tying. From early morning until late at night, I worked harder than at any other time in my life.

What I didn't expect, along with all the added parenting responsibilities, was the ridiculous amount of paperwork. Multi-page school registration applications. Forms for individual education plans to address their learning disabilities. Applications for a private speech and language therapist. At least thirty or forty pages to register as a guardian with the county social services department. Triplicate forms for healthcare coverage. Then more stacks of medical-records paperwork once I tracked down the rare doctor, dentist, and optometrist who accepted said coverage. Not to mention transportation forms, childcare forms, therapy forms, and legal forms.

Sandwiching every individual piece of paper were hours of online research, phone calls, and face-to-face appointments. I thought it would never end.

I'd love to tell you how infinitely kind and patient I was during that first oh-so-chaotic year. How, after a hard day's work, we circled up to play ring-around-the-rosy, sing songs, do family devotions, and hold hands.

It wasn't that way for us. We had sweet moments, of course. And like a trail of bread crumbs, those moments of refreshment led me through our forest. In between sweet crumbs, however, it was all about survival. Plain and simple.

My house had been hijacked. Overnight, everything from my

schedule to my kitchen plates had been disrupted and destroyed. The life I'd had before the littles came didn't exist anymore. What remained I didn't recognize. I felt out of place in my own house.

Like taking in walls covered in red marker, I looked at the mess and cringed.

~

Art often appears in the most unexpected places.

A short time after the marker on my walls, I stumbled across beauty in a place I didn't anticipate. It started with a simple internet search. A couple of hours later, I learned something that changed my perspective.

In 1874, on the streets of an art-loving Paris, the Anonymous Society of Painters, Sculptors, Printmakers decided to organize an art exhibition. This group of independent artists included notables like Camille Pissarro, Pierre-Auguste Renoir, and Claude Monet. Their purpose? To declare their independence from the more academic art world's penchant for structure and style.

Instead of clean lines and soft shades, these artists used shocking color and blurred edges. They emphasized light and shadow, and pure, unblended color. This gave their art movement, spontaneity, and texture. At least in the eyes of the artist.

This new technique, however, made patrons uncomfortable. Critics complained their work appeared unfinished, sloppy. Merely an impression of what is, rather than a depiction of it.

Thus the birth of impressionism.

Monet's *Impression, Sunrise*, part of the 1874 exhibition, remains one of the era's finest. When standing close to the painting, maybe two feet away, the colors don't blend well, appearing abrupt and unkempt. And the yellow-orange sun appears too shocking for the blue-green hues of the French harbor, Le Havre. Thus critics complained it was merely an "impression," not a finished or complete work.

If the naysayers had taken a few steps back, however, I wonder if *Impression, Sunrise* might've become a place of imagination. With a cushion of distance, the slashes of Monet's bright colors blend and move, causing the harbor to appear so real you can almost see the boats bob on the current. You picture an old man, bearded and gray, sitting in his vessel, oars in hand, and you wonder about his story.

Ultimately, your opinion of impressionism depends on where you stand to take in the view. You will end up a critic or a fan as a result of your vantage point.

I couldn't help but think the same is true when a life endures a shocking change of events. Such as an unexpected cancer diagnosis and the addition of three children.

I have a bad habit of standing too close to my circumstances. Proximity provides me a sense of control. If I can roll up my sleeves, manage all the details, and mop up the messes, I feel better about things. I want structure and predictability.

But standing close enough to control also means seeing every brushstroke in point-blank detail. I see flaws with shocking clarity. Notice the way my missteps bump and bleed into others, and theirs into me. Rather than a story filled with possibilities, I see abrupt slashes of unwanted color, all of the many scenarios I didn't expect and can't control.

When I do this, stand nose-to-canvas to evaluate the art, the intensity is too much. I'm overwhelmed by my life. Disappointed in it.

This creates a fascinating paradox. Life, in all its shocking unpredictability, is to be lived up close, personal. We are to hover within arm's length, interact and connect with real people and stories close enough to inhale, taste, and touch.

But although life is to be lived as such, its value can't be measured from the same proximity. To do so will create an obsession with the countless errant details. Instead, to make peace with a life, to see it as art, requires a stepping back. With a gentle buffer of space, the slashes of color blend into the workings of an overall whole.

Only then do we see boats bobbing on the waves and a new sun rising in the sky. Spontaneity and randomness show evidence of artistic design. Though appearing undone, it hints that imperfection could turn into the makings of an incredible story.

And perhaps a breathtaking work of art.

~

I don't recall any other time in life when I felt so exhausted. Most days were marked by my watching the clock move toward the littles' 7:30 p.m. bedtime. And most nights I went to bed an hour after they did. Even so, when the alarm screamed at me the next morning, it was all I could do to drag my weary body out of bed.

By 7:30 a.m., day after day, the littles bounced into the kitchen with more energy and activity than a three-ring circus. I'm a morning person, through and through. But the volume was too much for me.

One morning in particular, the thought of enduring another day brought me to the edge of madness. Even after a full night's sleep, I had nothing to give. Merely the thought of making breakfast made me want to collapse and cry.

I poured myself a cup of coffee, cradled it. Then, needing a pep talk even more than my dark roast, I opened my NIV Bible and the small *Jesus Calling* book sitting next to it. I needed something to hang on to, to give me a jolt of reassurance to make it through another day.

Through the words of Sarah Young, this is what he poured into my cup: "Glorifying and enjoying me is a higher priority than maintaining a tidy, structured life. Give up your striving to keep everything under control—an impossible task and waste of precious energy."[37]

Not what I wanted to hear, but what I needed. My desire for a tidy life was simply that—my desire. This was the demand I made of myself and the people in my life, including God. But it was a demand God had no intention of meeting. Instead, he soothed my angst with a hint of freedom: *I never wanted nor promised a tidy life. I want you. And I promised me.*

In the span of two phone calls, I lost every semblance of order. Each morning I woke up to unknowns: Is the cancer really gone? What if it comes back? How long will the littles be with us? How will I do this for another fourteen years if they stay? And if they leave, how will I let them go? In the absence of answers to these questions, life turned anything but tidy.

From that vantage point, I saw a mess to maintain rather than a story to unfold. I wanted a mouth that didn't hurt, children who behaved, a calendar I could count on. In short, I wanted structure and comfort, predictability and perfection. As a result, I almost missed the art taking shape.

My addiction to comfort and control—for both myself and my circumstances—had become both idol and crutch. It's what I pursued and reached for, with both hands and endless effort. But all the striving came with a cost. In my attempts to manage my life, I missed out on the vibrancy of it.

I wanted to do right by the littles. I wanted to make up for all they'd lost, to be the mother they always needed but didn't have. Even so, the grief I felt at my changing family was real and valid. Much was lost in the gaining of three children. This calling we accepted was neither easy nor glamorous.

Children are a heritage from the Lord, the Bible says. Yes. One thousand times, *yes.* The gain was a worthy and holy one. But to disregard the losses that came as a result is to dishonor the significance of the exchange made. And only in grieving could I free myself to keep living.

Like impressionistic art on the streets of Paris, it was all about vantage point. As I grieved, I had to step back from the canvas of my life—the flaws I resented in myself and the unanswered questions I couldn't control—so I could see the movement of an incredible story. In changing my perspective, I discovered that my infernal perfectionism also provided me the energy needed to give my best to three children who needed it. My obsession with structure and schedules ended up being the safety the children desperately craved. And the cancer—the wretched cancer that paralyzed me with fear—ended up becoming the source of compassion for three children always terrified about tomorrow.

Against all odds, I started to see the flaws as a necessary part of the canvas of my story. Then, only then, did I begin to make peace with the marker on the walls.

And so, with revelation sinking deep into my flawed self, I stepped back from the canvas to take in the art from the vantage point of the Artist.

Coffee mug in hand, I read these words: "To him who is able to keep you from stumbling and to present you before his glorious presence without fault and with great joy . . ."[38]

To him who is able to keep me from stumbling.

Days or weeks later, on yet another day far removed from

the dining-room art exhibition, Princess bounced into the kitchen with another piece of artwork. She held it out, eyes bright as she waited for my approval.

"Look what I made, Mommy!"

Mommy. She called me Mommy.

"Show me. What have you got?" I reached for her art, placed it on the counter to take a proper look.

A white piece of paper, with flowers, grass, a big yellow sun, and eight stick figures drawn in a line. At the end, one black and perfectly drawn stick dog.

At the top of her paper, she'd written two words: "My family."

Be still, my heart.

It took a child's colored-pencil drawing for me to finally see. A story is more than a neat and tidy house with all the laundry done and dishes put away. And a life is more than the limits of my best efforts. A real family—a well-lived life—is found in the marker on the walls, the self-inflicted haircuts, and well-used books. Children who sometimes make too much noise and a mom and dad who sometimes lose their patience. Eight stick figures (and one stick dog) who hold hands in the grass and weather the mess.

Can't see it? Then you're probably standing too close, where the flaws and misfortunes interfere with the view.

Instead, step back. Allow yourself to see beyond the chaos to the beautiful story taking shape.

One person's mess is Another's canvas. It's simply a matter of vantage point.

CHAPTER 22

Until We're Home

I discovered later, and I'm still discovering right up to this moment, that it is only by living completely in this world that one learns to have faith.... By this-worldliness I mean living unreservedly in life's duties, problems, successes and failures, experiences and perplexities. In so doing we throw ourselves completely into the arms of God, taking seriously not our own sufferings, but those of God in the world—watching with Christ in Gethsemane. That, I think, is faith.

—DIETRICH BONHOEFFER,
Letters and Papers from Prison

FROM THE FIRST DAY I HELD MY SON, JACOB, IN MY ARMS—ON the Valentine's Day of his birth—I sang to him. One song in particular.

"Sing the star song, Mommy!" he begged each night, after dinner-eating, teeth-brushing, and book-reading.

I had a tough time saying no to him back then, during those two or three years when only single mother and son made up our tired, worn family. As we cuddled on his bed, covered by striped blue sheets and the dark of night, he tucked his little boy head against my shoulder while I sang his song:

He numbers each and every star
And calls them all by name
He counts them one by one and sees
That they are still in place
If he cares for every star
Then he sees right where you are
You can trust you'll never fall
From his embrace[39]

We'd both lost on love. My boy, his biological father and intact family. Me, my dream and first love. So mother and son held each other in the dark and sang of a love that would not let us go. A love we could not be separated from, not by "trouble or hardship or persecution or famine or nakedness or danger or sword."[40] These words were my earth, and I hoped my son would discover them to be as sure for him.

When my marriage to Troy added two more little boys, I continued to sing, but to a larger audience. Over time, other songs joined our repertoire, but the "star song" became their favorite, as it'd been ours.

As my boys grew, the song became more a prayer, filled with the gutsy urgency I felt as I watched them inching toward manhood. I knew, from painful experience, that life didn't always turn out as planned. As much as I wanted to promise them the moon, I couldn't deliver even tomorrow. The future sat in hands that weren't mine.

The first time I read John 10:10, I thought I'd won the lottery: "I have come that they may have life, and have it to the full."

Yes, please. I'll take two.

Like pulling up to a Starbucks drive-through, I gave God my order and expected him to fill it. I wasn't asking for much. I could've prayed for millions of dollars, shiny new toys, and expansive, beautiful houses. Instead, I prayed more noble and worthy prayers, churchy ones.

For a faithful husband.

For a houseful of children who adored me.

For a solid church family, and years of rewarding service.

What kind of God wouldn't want to make those dreams come true?

My prayers received unexpected answers. My ministry-loving husband turned out to love addiction more than me. Divorce launched me from ministry into single motherhood. Adoring children turned adolescents, making our home a place of conflict. Our "solid" church family split down the middle. And cancer proved impossible to predict or avoid.

"I have come that they may have life, and have it to the full." That's what he said, those exact words. But a full life doesn't mean an easy life. In many cases, it means just the opposite.

And so, long before I became mother to three more children, I sang of stars and the God who counts them to three little boys who needed to know he'd never let them go.

~

A family vacation. That's what we needed.

Troy and I packed up our newish SUV (seven passenger, only slightly smaller than the Blue Beast) with the littles, the youngest of our bigs, an exhausted dog, and enough clothes to last a solid week. Then we pointed west and drove toward my parents' house.

Let me tell you, you have not lived until you've driven thirteen hours through Colorado, Utah, and Nevada in a cramped SUV with six people and a dog. But on the other side of that goodness sat Mimi and Papa's house. Quiet and welcoming. Clean. And with a stocked refrigerator, swimming pool, and built-in babysitting. Worth it.

The littles had never experienced a family vacation, didn't know what it was. It was my pleasure to induct them into the experience. For a solid week, we did nothing but sleep, eat, and play. We swam until we tired of the sun. We ate ice cream and watched Disney movies. We played games, shared tickle fights, and colored countless pages in Mimi's coloring books.

We spent our last full day in the pool, soaking up those last moments of sunshine. I sat on a stretched-out beach towel with my legs dangling in the water. The sun warmed me head to toe, but not as much as the sounds of my littles as they rediscovered their childhood.

Look at me!

Watch me jump!

See how good I swim?

Princess appeared to enjoy the day even more than her siblings. For hours, she giggled and splashed, never tiring, never complaining. Again and again she jumped into the pool, splashing me in the process and laughing at her accomplishment.

Then, sandwiched between squeals and jumps so I almost missed it, she stood at the side of the pool and looked at me. Arms thrust wide and with a smile to match, she announced to the entire world, "You're the best mom and dad ever!" With that, she leapt into the air and cannonballed into the water.

Her proclamation stunned me. Seven precise and costly words. Ones she meant with every ounce of her being.

Of course, sitting there at the side of the pool, I knew she was wrong. We're not the best mom and dad ever. In time, she'd discover I'm flawed and broken. Impatient, sometimes stern, often too busy and overwhelmed.

Still, after teenagers, it was nice to hear. Sometimes I get it right. Sometimes I play and laugh and kiss wet foreheads with a whispered, "I love you, sweet girl." Sometimes I stop working so hard to be perfectly grown up and instead satisfy myself with simply living and loving. And when I do, when I get over all the flaws and instead lean into what is, a lost little girl cheers from the side of a swimming pool.

Which is why, several hours later, after I'd tucked her into bed, the sound of her crying pierced me.

We'd said prayers, kissed heads, and pulled covers under chins. Then a half hour later, I heard crying. One of the girls. At first I stiffened, thought it was another bedtime delay tactic. *I'm thirsty! I have to go potty! My head hurts!* I'd heard it all before and prepped to deliver a warning.

By some miracle, I stopped long enough to think: she's the last to cry. Of all my littles, she's the least likely to use her tears for attention or manipulation. But that night she heaved, struggling to catch a breath before another sob shook her.

Mercy. A holy nudge softened my impulse. Instead of correction, she needed comfort. As I entered her room and sat on the side of her bed, I pushed wild strands of blond hair away from her flushed face.

"What's wrong, sweetheart?"

I asked, but she couldn't answer. Her chest shook. I waited, caressed wet cheeks, hoping my presence calmed her pain.

"Honey, what's wrong?" I tried again, concern urging me forward. "You have to tell me what's going on. Why are you upset?"

She inhaled, then braved an answer. "I'm ... going ... to ... miss ... Mimi and Papa!"

Another seven words. Precise, costly. Delivered with a heart-splitting wail.

Now I understood. The following morning, we'd leave. After eight days of play, we'd pack suitcases, say goodbyes, and turn toward home. To a little girl, the week had played out like a fairytale. Tomorrow, the dream would end.

Hence, she grieved.

I moved her small frame to the far edge of the bed, straightened the soft pink and white sheets, and settled her teddy bear under her other arm. Then I crawled beneath her blanket and slid my arm underneath her head. She felt warm and damp, spent from grief. I could feel her body shake beneath my arms. As I held on, she cried.

Lying there, swallowed by the dark, I thought of all the goodbyes my girl had endured. Her mom. Her dad. Countless relatives and friends, homes and beds. Hers had been a childhood marked by loss. Before she was old enough to start school, she'd lived in more places than most adults encounter in a lifetime. In the absence of stability, she grew to view life as unsafe. Unpredictable.

But then that day in the Walmart parking lot. The day she and her siblings joined our family. Not a perfect family, not a family without flaws and failures, but eight people determined to stick together. In a home with bedrooms and beds. Food at least three times a day. Familiar faces tucking her in at night and waiting for her to come down to breakfast in the morning. And a sweet, unforgettable family vacation to Mimi and Papa's house.

I brushed her hair with my hand and tried to soothe the pain I knew she felt. Tomorrow's goodbye felt all too familiar. She'd already said too many goodbyes, and I wondered if she feared yet another might follow. One that would take her away from us and back into chaos.

Please, God. Don't take her away from me! I couldn't let myself think about it, or I'd end up weeping along with my girl. But even as I held her, I knew the truth: the future was beyond my reach. No one could promise me my littles were here to stay. Today, yes. Tomorrow? No one knew. Situations like ours come with unparalleled complication, influenced by the whims of biological parents and a court system that doesn't always mete out justice.

I knew this. From the very first day, I knew I could lose them. At first, I tried to hold them at arm's length, fulfill their needs without falling in love. But it's impossible to mother little ones without the heart intertwining with theirs. Love grows through our best attempts at fences.

I pulled her tighter, noticed her cries had softened to sighs. How I loved this girl! More than anything, I wanted to promise her the moon. To guard her against loss and deliver a pain-free future.

But I wouldn't make promises I couldn't keep.

The irony? Cancer taught me this. Eight months before she arrived, an unexpected diagnosis forced me to face the undoneness of life. Not an easy revelation when life hangs in the balance. But in my wrestling for peace, I'd found a peace that transcends control, that runs deeper and stronger than any assurances or answers.

The presence of a God who would see me through.

Now, holding a shaking girl in my arms, I saw the past two years with clarity. This wasn't about cancer, or about the losses my littles had endured. Those were details, scenery, but not the bigger story. This was about making peace with an unexpected life. As if divine foresight had seen the moment at hand, I had to learn to release my terror so I could help a little girl release her own. I had to learn to embrace the unfinished, undone, upside-down places so three children in the middle of their own chaos could find the better story.

I felt my girl shudder in my arms. She didn't need my empty promises and false reassurances.

There, in the dark of Mimi and Papa's house, I remembered the star song. It was long retired after my boys had become young men; I pulled it out and dusted it off. She needed those words like she needed air. Maybe I did too.

A child—a grown-up—can endure most any horror, as long as we know we're not alone. The touch and presence of another makes the difference. A hand held, hair caressed, a tear touched. As Corrie ten Boom, Nazi concentration camp survivor, once remarked, "Happiness is not dependent on happenings, but on relationship in the happenings."[41]

Even so, human relationships have limits. They can't redeem, save, or rescue. Which is why my girl needed to know there is another, an infinite, healing, redeeming God whose love for her is both inescapable and inexhaustible. Who can heal all things broken, and to whom she'll never need to say goodbye. Not just for today, but for all the tomorrows I cannot predict or control.

"How about I sing you a song?" I whispered.

She sniffled, nodded.

I took a deep breath and began.

Epilogue

> *The point is to live everything. Live the questions now. Perhaps you will then gradually, without noticing it, live along some distant day into the answer.*
>
> —RAINER MARIA RILKE, *Letters to a Young Poet*

THE IRONY ABOUT WRITING MEMOIR—OR AT LEAST WRITING A *current* memoir—is that life keeps happening even as you write about it. It's like trying to work on a moving desk. The plot changes faster than you can pen it.

It's now been almost four years since the first phone call, well over three since the second. Some days I feel far removed from those early days of near drowning, when my life capsized. Most of the time, however, I realize I'm still suspended in the deep end of the pool. Not drowning, per se, but fully aware of the possibility of going under.

Perhaps this is the norm for a family with six children. Those of you likewise raising entire ball teams and pom squads will have to let me know. Or maybe our chaos is unique to blended families and to parents loving children who have special needs and who show evidence of post–traumatic stress disorder and reactive attachment disorder. I'm more inclined to believe the latter.

A good friend, Melissa, recently asked, "How are you hanging in there?"

I almost always chuckle at this question. It's a strange one, considering our "adjustment phase" is now pushing four years. But Melissa gets it. Crises like ours don't follow a timeline. Transition isn't something you add to your to-do list one day and check off on another. You walk it through one day at a time, baby. One day at a time. Then, by some miracle, a morning dawns when you open your eyes, feel the warmth of hope, and discover you're farther along than you thought.

I answered Melissa with the same frank honesty she's come to expect from me.

"Well, let me put it this way. We're out of the ER and into the ICU. Still in critical condition, but stabilized."

I'd always believed that the goal of the faith life is wholeness, to live outside the hospital doors. I aimed to be healthy, strong, full of hope and optimism. If any of these ingredients were missing, the secret was to discipline and pray my way back to health.

Without a doubt, those of us who love Jesus have every reason for all of those things. Strength. Hope. And certainly optimism. We've been given salvation, redemption, and a promise of heaven. Good cause to celebrate.

But in my pursuit of personal perfection and the ideal life, I'd neglected to take into account a powerful and undeniable factor: humanness. Somehow I tricked myself into believing I could rise above my fallibility with enough effort, control, and good intention. With enough exercise and church attendance and good old-fashioned hard work.

Then cancer. The ultimate evidence of my mortality. And three hurting children. The flesh-and-blood proof of human frailty. Cancer and kids put me in the hospital, both literally and figuratively. I couldn't fix either one, and for a while I believed that meant I'd failed.

Until I discovered that joy and strength and hope are possible even in the sick ward. Maybe more so. I learned that faith in the middle of the unknowns is the only real kind. And peace can't be found in the past or the future, but only in a Person, and in whom you believe him to be, today. And an unexpected life, as difficult and undone as it might be, could end up becoming the life you've been searching for all along.

My story continues to unfold. Even today, as I write these final words, I could give additional pages of evidence of how complicated, unexpected, and difficult it continues to be. At times I wish it were easier, I won't lie. I'd give anything for a normal, boring day. But I'm not sure normal would keep me kneeling.

As of today, we're still a family of eight. This may stay the same, or it may change. I have zero guarantees. For now, our littles sleep in their same beds, wake up to the same alarm clock, eat breakfast at the same counter, and hear "I love you" from the same mama and daddy. Each August, I fill out triplicate stacks of paperwork as I register them for school. Every time, I wonder if I'll have the privilege of doing the same the following year.

It's an undone place, and I hate it. It's limbo in its most painful form, with my family—and my fragile heart—on the line. I hover between potential outcomes, not knowing how it will turn out. At times, I catch myself worrying about the what-ifs, trying to predict and prepare. It takes effort to lay it down, to stop trying to fit all of the puzzle pieces together. For now, God has asked me to trust him with the result. To love without restraint, even knowing a day may come when I'll have to say goodbye. I'm banking on the fact that, if and when the time comes, my Father will know how to glue this mama's broken heart back together. After all, he's done it countless times before.

As for cancer? It came back. But not as I expected.

First, it showed up last summer when my dad, the carpenter who taught me never to give up, went in for a checkup. We'd been vacationing together only a couple of weeks before. After we left, my mom noticed his skin turning a strange shade of yellow. At first the doctor thought it was hepatitis A or a blocked bile duct. It turned out to be the latter, because of tumors.

Pancreatic cancer. Not what I expected. Again. This time, however, I didn't unravel. Not because it wasn't serious and I wasn't concerned. It was, and I was. But something about my own life-and-death journey, years before, prepared me to walk this one. I'd learned that fear has only as much rope as I give it. And to get ahead of the doctors and the days is to borrow unnecessary trouble. "Who of you by worrying can add a single hour to your life?" Jesus asked.[42] A valid question, a powerful one. Like the Israelites with their manna, we needed to walk my dad's cancer journey one day at a time, trusting God for another manna delivery tomorrow.

But that wasn't to be the last of the unexpected. Only a few months later, as Dad neared the end of his chemo treatments and we believed he had his cancer licked, a thick, painful lesion on the same left side of my tongue demanded a second look. I did my best to heal it, to get it to go away. But in the end my efforts didn't matter. I found myself again on the examination table in the familiar patient room as Dr. Forrester performed yet another biopsy. Five days later, during which I once again hovered in limbo, the phone rang.

Yes, the cancer came back. More serious this time, requiring a six-hour surgery, tissue graft, neck dissection, and lymph node removal. Even so, even with all the pain, terrifying oncology conversations, and long, agonizing weeks of recovery, fear didn't overwhelm. Instead, a sweet, palpable peace.

Call it a move of divine orchestration, but this second diagnosis showed up the same week I worked on edits for this book. Hours before the phone rang, I read through the pages of this story, remembering with awe God's nearness in that season of horrific darkness. Then, in the moments after I hung up the phone and faced full the enormity of this new challenge, he eased my tears with the same inexhaustible truths I'd lived years before.

Looking back on those wearying weeks, I'm relieved God saw fit to blanket me with an extra measure of peace. Although I had no way of knowing it at the time, I'd need it more than ever before in the weeks to follow. A far greater storm was yet to come.

Six short weeks after my surgery, while I was yet consumed with my physical and emotional recovery, my sweet daddy likewise received an unwanted phone call. The cancer we'd all believed he'd soundly beaten returned. Only this time it was inoperable. All those radiation treatments, chemo appointments, and healing prayers to no avail. One to two years, the doctor said. If we were lucky. Regardless, the prognosis was plain: terminal.

My dad—our Papa—called me the day he found out. I'll never forget the heaviness in his voice, the weight of sadness as he spoke words he knew would break my heart. But more than our shared emotion, I'll never forget the conversation that followed. You see, we needed each other that day in a way few can understand. Father and daughter, two undone Jesus-lovers fighting cancer together. Holding onto each other and our faith with both hands. Cheering each other on, praying each other through. Considering the horrific circumstances, you'd think our phone time would've been spent commiserating. Certainly we had every reason to be despondent, angry even. This wasn't how the story was supposed to end! This wasn't what we'd prayed for! Of course, my time of wrestling and anger would come, later. But for that day, with a father on one end of the phone and a daughter on the other, we simply cried together and took inventory of our blessed and beautiful lives. Our joint cancer diagnoses wasn't a nasty string of bad luck. It was a tender provision.

"Even if I don't live another day, I've had such a good life," he told me. "I'm so blessed!" His voice carried certainty. Peace. And calm, even as he cried. He trusted the God who'd always loved him. And in hearing his words, I found new courage to do the same.

Three months after that phone call, far less time than any of us imagined, my sweet daddy flew home to his Jesus. To this day, I have no answers to my question of why God didn't intervene. I don't understand why he didn't step in and protect us from yet one more loss. It makes no sense to my limited perception, and my heart still aches from the pain of it. Even so, even as this daughter who misses her daddy cries rivers of tears, I hear another Father drawing me back to the love that will not fail, even when the world turns upside-down:

Nothing will be able to separate you from me, Michele. Nothing!

It's seems too easy, doesn't it? To claim to find this kind of anchor in the face of unbelievable tumult? On the contrary, it isn't easy at all. Making peace with the unexpected life isn't some trite, Christian cliche. It isn't a beautiful string of words that looks nice and shiny hanging around my neck. The kind of peace that weathers a furious squall by sleeping in the boat is both hard earned and God delivered. One story—and serving of manna—at a time. And by the mercy and grace of the one who walked me through all the storms leading up to this one, I can finally say, even as the rain soaks my face, "I am convinced."[43] He will not let me go.

As for all the other undone places, the list is far too long. In the past several weeks, we've had broken bones, car accidents, busted pipes, and all other manner of parenting and marital challenges. It's the way this crazy life rolls. Part of the deal when you exit the birth canal and give that first lusty cry.

It's an undone life. But I don't have to be undone by it. Stressed? Yes, quite often. Exhausted? You bet. Do I cry, rant, and sometimes act like a toddler on a sugar high four hours past bedtime? Yes, yes, and yes.

I am an impossible, stubborn, gloriously imperfect woman. From my bad hair-color job to the piles of unlaundered clothes. From my list of missed appointments to the kids' impressive collection of tardy slips. From my marriage in progress to the children who still think it's okay to use their arm as a napkin. From my desperate closet prayers to the long days of doubt.

I'm undone. Hungry, questioning, searching, struggling. Not even close to polished and pristine.

But I'm breathing. And believing. And loving this crazy, unexpected, and imperfect life.

Several months ago, while at my parents' house, we took the littles to California. They'd never seen the ocean before, didn't understand the vastness of the water or the power of the waves.

When we arrived, the girls squealed in delight and ran down the sand of Huntington Beach. Unafraid, they jumped into the waves, then screamed and exited with surprise at the cold. Even so, their faces filled with mirth. For the next hour they giggled and played in both sand and surf.

Jack approached the ocean with more caution, holding a grown-up hand and keeping quiet. He could see the intensity of the water, felt the strength of the tide as wave after wave crested his feet and then threatened to pull him back out into its depths.

For the longest time, he simply stood there, watching rather than playing. I could see the conflict within, his desire to play warring with his fear of danger.

His was a valid battle, because the ocean is dangerous. It can't be managed or controlled. And sometimes, even though you ache for it to be otherwise, it takes a person under.

But the ocean is also a place of adventure and thrill, of deep belly laughter and memories you'll never forget.

But only for those who dare to dive in.

This is the choice you and I face each day, as we wrestle with forgiveness and cancer, complicated relationships and unknown outcomes. Retreat or dive? Watch or live?

To stay on the beach is to miss out on the ocean. It's safer there, on your beach chair far from the unpredictability of the water. But it isn't really living. Instead, dare to *lean in.* Allow the water to drench and cover and clean. Experience it, savor it, *enjoy it.*

Why? Because this is where your story and mine are written, right here with so much at stake and even more possible. And with an incredible Author pulling it all together for the perfect end. Ours is a God who heals all things sick. Who redeems all things lost. Who brings orphans together in unusual families. And who weaves all frail and broken things into a glorious overall whole. A story. His story.

And the best news of all?

When we reach the final page, regardless of what happens between now and then, hope wins.

So go ahead. You've got nothing to lose and everything to gain.

Dive.

Acknowledgments

THERE'S A STORY I TELL OF MY SON'S FIRST CROSS-COUNTRY RACE.

Only thirteen at the time, Jacob didn't yet understand the agony of a runner's journey. He simply wanted the thrill of the finish. Thus, when the day of that first race came, I planted myself deep in the middle of the course and readied myself to cheer like only a half-crazy mama can.

For years now, I've been running a tough race. Looking back, I see clearly the faces of those who lined my course, cheering when both courage and strength waned. This book made it to the finish as a result of these people, as much as any effort of my own.

To Carolyn McCready, this really must begin with you. Two years ago, over delicious hors d'oeuvres and a delightful cabernet, your eyes shone when I shared my story. With grace, you challenged me to find the metaphor, to dig deep and uncover the golden thread. Turns out you gave excellent advice. Thank you for your belief, prayers, and always-keen insight. But thank you, especially, for those shining eyes.

To Brian Phipps, Londa Alderink, and the rest of the Zondervan team: I'm not sure how I ended up with such stellar colaborers, but I'm thrilled. The months between signing contract and seeing book on shelf came with a second diagnosis, surgery, and unknowns none of us could've anticipated. You handled the unexpected with grace and efficiency, and always made it about both my healing and the Healer. Thank you for that.

To Brian Scheer and Joy Groblebe of the Frontline Group, my two-person army: Only you (and Troy) know how many times I nearly walked away. Like Moses' Aaron and Hur, you kept me in the battle when I didn't have the strength to fight. You may be my managers, but you are foremost my dear friends.

To my agent, Andrew Wolgemuth: The first time we met over crepes, I could see your love for Jesus as clearly as your warm smile. You're a fine agent, and I'm honored to partner with you. But more than your expertise, I love that we share our First Love.

To Ken and Diane Davis: I had no idea how much my life would change the day I met you and the Dynamic Communicators International team. I thought I was signing up for a part-time job. How grossly I underestimated what our God would do! Your influence on my heart and family runs deep. Thank you for loving me enough to push me forward.

Michael Hyatt: You and Gail are far more than my coworkers. For all the countless ways, both seen and unseen, that you have advocated for this project, prayed for our family, and cheered me on, I am in your debt. I'm so glad we're friends.

To Robbie Iobst, Melissa Caddell, Danica Favorite-MacDonald, Kay Day, Loretta Oakes, and Amy Thedinga, my longtime writing friends who courageously read through page after disastrous page of early copy: Lord have mercy, "long-suffering" doesn't cover it. Somehow you saw the gold through the dross, in both the manuscript and me. You should be sainted.

To Greg and Becky Johnson and Lindsey O'Connor, fellow word lovers and friends: It's impossible to overstate how much I esteem you, treasure you. Not only did you deliver countless meals and pep talks while I juggled surgery, recovery, motherhood, and writing, you believed in me and this book from the first word. Not once did you sway. I will never forget.

To those who slogged through the first draft, and the many friends and family who allowed me to share their stories: Marion Roach Smith (who edited the entire first copy, with brilliance), Rhonda, Don, Dana, Bev, Greg, Evan, Danny, Cassie, Mark, Erika, Damian, Alece. And to Kathi, Renee, and Crystal, who generously share their expertise, heart, and affirmation with a deep and divine sister-love.

To my parents, Loren and Deanna Trethewey: There is not room enough here to give you adequate thanks. But I will say this. You have given me two immeasurable gifts: (1) Belief that I could do anything. *Anything*. And (2) faith. Both made what you now hold possible. A princess couldn't ask for more. I love you.

To Tyler, Ryan, and Jacob, the boys who filled the first pages of my mothering story with ample material (and then gave courageous permission for me to share it): How I love you! No one has made me cry harder or laugh more than you. You are God's answer to the grade-school prayers of a girl who wanted nothing more than to be a mom, in all the glorious imperfections of it. I wouldn't change a thing.

To my littles, Princess, Peanut, and Jack: Although grief and loss brought us together, it is the grace and love of God that make us a family. He will redeem all things lost, heal all things broken. It is my honor to be your second mama. How much do I love you? Yes, thaaaaat much! Will I ever stop? No, *never*. You will be "oaks of righteousness, a planting of the LORD for the display of his splendor" (Isa. 61:3).

Troy: Just typing your name tightens my throat. You, more than anyone, see my undoneness. I'm in-progress, unfinished, immature, and quite possibly undermedicated. And yet you see something in me worth fighting for, worth loving. I will never understand it, but I receive it. And I offer the gift right back to you. Oh, and one more thing. Remember that Mother's Day laptop? Turns out you were right. I love to write.

Now. At the risk of sounding like a star receiving an Oscar, I have one last thank you.

Jesus, from the moment I met you I've been undone. You have pursued me, confused me, led me, wrecked me, and, above all, loved me. I have no idea what's next, and sometimes the truth of that scares me. But this I do know: I am yours. And you will not let me go. "If your Presence does not go with us, do not send us up from here.... *Now show me your glory*." (Exod. 33:15, 18).

Notes

1. Exod.16:4.
2. Stuart K. Hine and Carl G. Boberg, "How Great Thou Art" (Carol Stream, IL: Hope Publishing Company).
3. Luke 15:11–32.
4. Luke 15:22–24.
5. Sam Keen. *To Love and Be Loved* (New York: Bantam-Random House, 1999).
6. John 20:19.
7. John 20:20–21.
8. See Luke 2:14.
9. Placide Cappeau and Adolphe Adam, "O Holy Night," 1847.
10. Isa. 9:6.
11. John 14:27.
12. 2 Cor. 4:16–18.
13. 2 Cor. 1:3–4.
14. 2 Cor. 12:7–8.
15. Luke 12:25.
16. 2 Cor. 12:9.
17. 2 Cor. 12:10.
18. Isa. 58:10.
19. Mark 8:34–36.
20. Heb. 11:1.
21. Luke 2:6–7.
22. Joseph Mohr and Franz Gruber, "Silent Night, Holy Night!" 1818.
23. John T. Cacioppo and William Patrick, *Loneliness: Human Nature and the Need for Social Connection* (New York: Norton, 2008), 52.

24. Isa. 49:15–16.

25. Isa. 61:1, 3.

26. Madeleine L'Engle, *Walking on Water: Reflections on Faith and Art* (New York: North Point Press, 1980), 55.

27. Rabbi Evan Moffic, "How We Turn Anger into Holiness," Beliefnet.com, October 2, 2013, *http://blog.beliefnet.com/truthsyoucanuse/2013/09/how-to-turn-anger-into-holiness.html#ixzz2g7vTGU5d*.

28. Luke 8:22.

29. Luke 8:24.

30. 2 Cor. 4:7–9, 18.

31. 2 Chron. 20:2–3.

32. 2 Chron. 20:12.

33. 2 Chron. 20:15.

34. Matt. 11:28–30.

35. 2 Chron. 20:17.

36. Timothy Keller, *The Prodigal God: Recovering the Heart of the Christian Faith* (New York: Penguin, 2008), 125.

37. Sarah Young, *Jesus Calling: Enjoying Peace in His Presence* (Nashville: Thomas Nelson, 2004), 178, June 19 entry.

38. Jude 24.

39. "What Can Separate You?" Babbie Mason/Donna Douglas © 1996 May Sun Music (Admin. by Word Music, LLC), Word Music, LLC, Did My Music. All rights reserved. Used with permission.

40. Rom. 8:35.

41. Corrie ten Boom with Jamie Buckingham, *Tramp for the Lord* (Washington, PA: CLC Publications, 2010), 145.

42. Luke 12:25.

43. Romans 8:37.

The Next Chapter ...

The story of Michele, Troy, and their family continues to unfold.

To catch up on their latest adventures—and maybe find a dash of hilarity and hope for your own—connect with Michele:

www.MicheleCushatt.com